'A lyrical, painful and yet hope-filled memoir...
Shattering, light-searching'
Observer

'Unputdownable... *My Name Is Why* is authentic and beautiful,
a potential game-changer in public attitudes to children raised in care.
It's about bureaucratic cruelty and what happens when love is absent.
Don't miss it'
The Times

'The great triumph of this work comes from its author's determination to
rail against what he rightly diagnoses as this institutionally endorsed
disremembering of black and marginalised experience. It is a searing and
unforgettable re-creation of the most brutal of beginnings'
Guardian

'Heartbreaking...Sissay has given us a blistering condemnation of the
"care" system – and his powerful voice asking "why?" is raised on behalf of
all children who have been its victims'
Daily Mail

'Remarkable...It is sensational stuff told with an elegant restraint that
leaves the reader feeling some of the hurt, bewilderment and anger that he
has endured...It is also a testament to Sissay himself
and his ability to survive, and later thrive'
Sunday Times

'A powerful memoir on growing up without parents and finding hope'
Sun

'Devastating'

i

'An extraordinary book, compelling and devastating and utterly humane'
PHILIPPE SANDS

'Everybody should read *My Name Is Why* – utterly devastating and yet
uplifting – you find yourself humbled by the spirit that is Lemn Sissay'
JACKIE KAY

'Compelling, moving and brilliant. If you find it difficult to see the world
from a child's viewpoint, this will help'
PHILIPPA PERRY

Also by Lemn Sissay

Poetry

Perceptions of the Pen
Tender Fingers in a Clenched Fist
The Fire People (ed.)
Morning Breaks in the Elevator
Rebel Without Applause
The Emperor's Watchmaker
Listener
Gold from the Stone

Drama

Skeletons in the Cupboard
Don't Look Down
Chaos by Design
Storm
Something Dark
Why I Don't Hate White People
Refugee Boy

My Name Is Why

A MEMOIR

Lemn Sissay

CANONGATE

First published in Great Britain, the USA and Canada in 2019
by Canongate Books Ltd, 14 High Street, Edinburgh EH1 1TE

Distributed in the USA by Publishers Group West
and in Canada by Publishers Group Canada

canongate.co.uk

1

British Library Cataloguing-in-Publication Data
A catalogue record for this book is available on
request from the British Library

ISBN 978 1 78689 234 8

Typeset in Garamond MT Std 12.5/16 pt by
Palimpsest Book Production Ltd, Falkirk, Stirlingshire

Printed and bound in Great Britain by Clays Ltd, Elcograf S.p.A.

MIX
Paper from
responsible sources
FSC® C018072
www.fsc.org

For
Yemarshet, Tsahaiwork, Teguest, Mehatem,
Giday, Abiyu, Mimi, Wuleta,
Catherine, David, Christopher, Sarah and Helen

The two most important days in your life are the day you are born and the day you find out why

—Anon., attributed to Mark Twain

I am the bull in the china shop
With all my strength and will
As a storm smashed the teacups
I stood still

PREFACE

At fourteen I tattooed the initials of what I thought was my name into my hand. The tattoo is still there but it wasn't my name. It's a reminder that I've been somewhere I should never have been. I was not who I thought I was. The Authority knew it but I didn't.

The Authority had been writing reports about me from the day I was born. My first footsteps were followed by the click clack clack of a typewriter: 'The boy is walking.' My first words were recorded, click clack clack: 'The boy has learned to talk.' Fingers were poised above a typewriter waiting for whatever happened next: 'The boy is adapting.'

Paper zipped from typewriters and into files. The files slipped into folders under the 'S' section of a tall metal filing cabinet. For eighteen years this process repeated over and over again. Click clack clack. Secret meetings were held. The folders were taken out and placed on tables surrounded by men and women from The Authority. Decisions were made: *Put him here, move him there. Shall we try drugs? Try this, try that.* After eighteen years of experimentation The Authority threw me out. It locked the doors securely behind me and hid the files in a data company called The Iron Mountain.

So I wrote to The Authority and hand-delivered the letter. The reply informed me I had to write to Customer Services. I wrote to Customer Services. Customer Services replied to say they were not permitted to release the files. The Authority placed me with incapable foster parents. It imprisoned me. It moved me from institution to institution. And yet now, at eighteen years old, I had no history, no witnesses, no family.

In 2015, following a thirty-year campaign to get my records, the Chief Executive of Wigan Council, Donna Hall, wrote me a letter. She had them. Within a few months I received four thick folders of documents marked 'A', 'B', 'C' and 'D'. Click clack clack. On reading them, I knew.

I took The Authority to court.

How does a government steal a child and then imprison him? How does it keep it a secret? This story is how. It is for my brothers and sisters on my mother's side and my father's side. This is for my mother and father and my aunts and uncles and for Ethiopians.

CHAPTER 1

Awake among the lost and found
The files left on the open floor
The frozen leaves on frosted ground
The frosted keys in a frozen door

Eighteen years of records written by strangers. All the answers to all my questions were here. Possibly. And yet, I feared what they'd reveal about me or what they'd reveal about the people who were entrusted with my care. What truths or untruths? Maybe I was loved. Maybe my mother didn't want me. Maybe it was all my fault. Maybe the bath taps in the bathroom were not electrified. Maybe that was false memory syndrome.

A friend burned her files when she received them from The Authority. Another can't look at hers to this day. I'll start by simply recording my reactions to the first early documents and we'll see how this unfolds.

ST. MARGARET'S HOUSE

GOOSE GREEN, WIGAN

(Affiliated to the Liverpool Board of Moral Welfare)

Telephone Wigan 42143

Warden and Chairman:
THE RECTOR OF WIGAN, THE HALL, WIGAN.

Treasurer:	Assist Treasurer:	Secretary:	Superintendent:
W. WILSON, Esq.,	Miss N. FAULKNER	Mrs. S. RENWICK,	Mrs. F. MALLOCH
379 Orrell Road	3 The Avenue,	59 Thornfield Road,	
Wigan.	Monument Park,	Thornton,	
	Wigan.	Liverpool, 23.	

30. 6. 64.

I hereby certify that
Lenira Sissey is free from
infectious disease'

L. Wenniad SRN
Sister

4

St Margaret's House was an institution for unmarried mothers 'affiliated to the Liverpool Board of Moral Welfare'. On 30 June 1967, State Registered Nurse L. Winnard wrote that 'Lemion Sissey' (misspelt) was 'free from infectious disease'. In a second note on the same day she recorded that the six-week-old baby – now 'Lemn Sissey'? – weighed nine pounds.

BABY LEMN SISSEY: age 6weeks

BORN: 21. 5. 67

BIRTH WEIGHT: 6lb 0oz

WEIGHT 30.6.67   9lb 0oz

PHENYLKETONURIA TEST   NEGATIVE

FEEDS:

Ostermilk NO1.   5 measures to water 6oz

4 hrly: Takes feeds Well.

Fed at 9.30A.   1.30P.   5.30P.   9.30PM

Takes a while to settle after 9.30P

feed: Wakes for night feed about

4 AM:

Buttocks satisfactory:

L Winnard SRN

5

In the letter below I'm six months old. At this point my mother is invisible.

DR. BARNARDO'S

Head Office: STEPNEY CAUSEWAY LONDON E.1.
AREA OFFICE: 248 UPPER PARLIAMENT STREET, LIVERPOOL 8
TELEPHONE: 051/709/6291

13th November, 1967.

OWW/PJ

OUR REF:

YOUR REF:

Dear Mr. Goldthorpe,

Further to your Department's enquiry regarding the possibility of our Adoption Department being able to place a part Ethiopian, part Greek baby boy for adoption. Our Senior Adoption Officer has written to us asking that she be supplied with full information about this baby; in particular, details of his background and whether Ethiopian means that he is negroid or not.

Yours sincerely,

O. W. Woods

N. Goldthorpe Esq.,
Children's Officer,
County Borough of Wigan,
Children's Department,
Civic Buildings,
Parson's Walk,
Wigan, Lancs.

O. W. Woods
Assistant Executive Officer
(Dictated by Mr. Woods and
signed in his absence)

6

And then there was this:

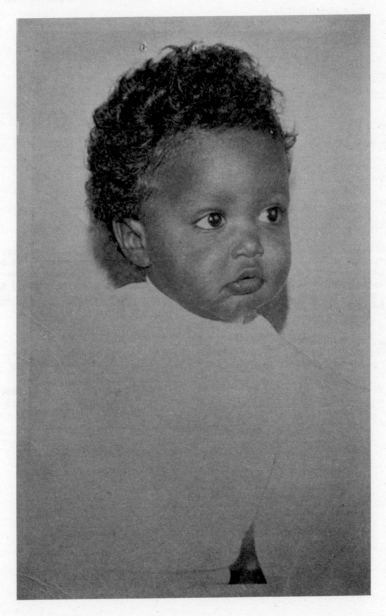

On the back of the photo it says:

NORMAN SISSAY

So my name has changed to Norman Sissay; I am supposed to be part Greek. An adoption agency asks whether 'Ethiopian means he is negroid or not'. This is the first time I have seen myself referred to as 'Norman Sissay'.

<u>Foster Child</u>   Lemn Sissay 21.5.67. Mother Ethiopian; putative father possibly Greek. Protestant.

It is anticipated that this will be a permanent foster home for Norman, and responsibility for payment of boarding out allowances and supervision will be retained by this Authority.

Yours sincerely,

<u>Children's Officer</u>

When the letter from which this extract is taken was written, I was almost eight months old. In England unmarried pregnant women or girls were placed in Mother and Baby homes like St Margaret's with the sole aim of harvesting their children, then the women were shipped back home to say they had been away on a little break. *A little break.* They were barely adults themselves. Many of them didn't understand the full implication of the word 'adoption'. They were sent home without their newborns after signing the adoption papers. They must have been bewildered and in shock at the loss of their first child. I found testaments online from people who lived near to St Margaret's.

It was very eerie in certain parts it really felt haunted.

I can remember being in the Billinge Maternity unit when one of the young girls from St Margaret's had her baby. The only visitor was a lady social worker and on the day mum and baby were due to leave, mum was taken away in one car (crying) and baby hurried away in another!

My mother would not sign the adoption papers for Norman Goldthorpe. So Norman Goldthorpe defied her and assigned me to 'long-term foster parents' Catherine and David Greenwood.

COUNTY BOROUGH OF WIGAN — CHILDREN'S DEPARTMENT

AGREEMENT OF FOSTER PARENTS

We/I _MR AND MRS GREENWOOD_
of _68 SWINTON CRESCENT, UNSWORTH, BURY_
having on the _3rd_ day of _January_ 19 _68_, received
from the Wigan County Borough Council (hereinafter called " the council "),
(NORMAN) LEMN SISSAY who was born on the
_21st_ day of _MAY_ 19 _67_, and whose religious
persuasion is _PROTESTANT_ into our/my home as a member of our/my family,
undertake that :—

1. We/I will care for _NORMAN_ and bring him/her up as
   we/I would a child of our/my own.

2. He/she will be brought up in, and will be encouraged to practise his/her religion.

3. We/I will look after his/her health and consult a doctor whenever he/she is ill and
   allow him/her to be medically examined at such times and places as the council may
   require.

4. We/I will inform the council immediately of any serious occurrence affecting the child.

5. We/I will at all times permit any person so authorised by the Secretary of State or by
   the council to see him/her and visit our/my home.

10

6. We/I will allow him/her to be removed from our/my home when so requested by a person authorised by the council of the county borough where we/I live.

7. If we/I decide to move, we/I will notify the new address to the council before we/I go.

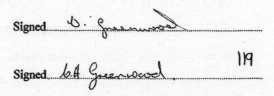

Signed .....O. Greenwood.....................

Signed .....bA Greenwood...................... 119

Date 3rd January 1968

I was 228 days old at the time. I must have been with them from at least 150 days old. My foster parents told me some years later that I was alone in the hospital because no one would adopt a 'coloured' baby. They said they chose me after praying to God and that my mother didn't want me.

Mr Goldthorpe was adamant that my name would be Norman. Norman means 'Man of the North'. The foster parents wanted to call me Mark from The Gospel of Mark, and their last name was Greenwood. My name was Norman Mark Greenwood. The Authority wouldn't officially acknowledge the name my foster parents called me. I am Norman Sissay in the files. The foster parents wouldn't acknowledge the name The Authority gave me. I was Norman Mark Greenwood and I knew no different. It was a land grab. But without my mother's signature on the adoption papers The Authority could not adopt me.

11

My mother must have been at her most vulnerable. She was pregnant and alone in a foreign country where she had come to study for a short period of time. Her college in the South of England sent her to the North of England to St Margaret's to deal with her pregnancy.

These places were baby farms. The mothers were the earth and the children were the crops. The church and state were the farmers and the adopting parents were the consumers. My mother was supposed to give birth and sign the adoption papers. She didn't. She wouldn't.

Testimony has come to light in national campaigns for unmarried mothers in England that in the 1960s coercion and subterfuge were used to get vulnerable women to sign the adoption papers. This is exemplified in the 2013 film *Philomena*.

My mother understood what adoption meant and would not sign. Her father – my grandfather – was dying in Ethiopia. She had little choice but to return to Ethiopia without me. With my name changed and the foster parents' identity hidden there was little chance she could find me if she wanted to.

I was three and a half years old when The Authority served a Notice on my mother via her church in Ethiopia to say that 'all the rights and powers of the parent of Lemn Sissay be vested in the local authority it appearing to this Authority that the parent has abandoned this child'. The document further states that: 'If not later than one month after the service of this notice, you shall serve a notice in writing on the Council objecting to the resolution, the resolution shall lapse on the expiration of fourteen days from the service of the notice of objection . . .'

She was given one month to object to the notice. Then she would have fourteen days to take The Authority to court, where she would have to prove to the court that she was a fit mother. The notice would have taken approximately a month to arrive in Ethiopia and another month for the letter to return. There were no direct flights from Addis Ababa to London. My mother would have had to fly from Addis Ababa to Athens and then from Athens to London. It was an impossible deadline. It was a set-up.

The Authority depends on the sleeping prejudice of assumptions because for this notice to have any premise we must *assume* that the mother didn't want the child or that she was unfit to keep the child.

Miss Y.Yemarshet Sissay
c/o Ethiopian Union Mission
P.O. Box 145,
Addisababa,
ETHIOPIA

COUNTY BOROUGH OF WIGAN
2 DEC 1970

COUNTY BOROUGH OF WIGAN

CHILDREN ACT 1948 AND CHILDREN

AND YOUNG PERSONS ACT 1963

NOTICE IS HEREBY GIVEN that on Tuesday the second day of December One

Thousand Nine Hundred and Seventy the Mayor Aldermen and Burgesses of the County

Borough of Wigan acting by the Council the Local Authority for the said County

igh (hereinafter called "the Council") did resolve:-

"That in pursuance of the powers contained in Section 2 (1) (b)
of the Children Act 1948 and Section 48 (1) of the Children
and Young Persons Act 1963, all the rights and powers of the
parent of Lemn Sissay be vested in the local authority it appearing
to this Authority that the parent has abandoned this child."

You are the mother of the aforesaid Lemn Sissay and therefore pursuant
to Section 2 (1) (b) of the Children Act 1948 and Section 48 (1) of the
Children and Young Persons Act 1963 your attention is drawn to the fact that
if not later than one month after the date of the service of this notice, you
shall serve a notice in writing on the Council objecting to the resolution,
the resolution shall lapse on the expiration of fourteen days from the
service of the notice of objection unless within that period the Council make
complaint to the Juvenile Court in which case the Court has power after hearing
the complaint to order that the resolution shall not lapse.

DATED this 2nd day of December, 1970.

My story begins without her or any knowledge of her.

14

CHAPTER 2

I will build an embassy
In your heart over time
There is a plot of land inside me
Build one in mine

The Greenwoods and I lived at Number 2, Osborne Road, where the swallows came each summer to nest in the eaves. It was a semi-detached house fronted by sandstone with a sheer, solid, red-brick gable-end wall flush to a cobbled street on the left. The garden at the front just about coped with a giant laburnum tree lunging from the bottom left corner. Google Dictionary tells me the laburnum is 'a small European tree which has hanging clusters of yellow flowers followed by slender pods containing poisonous seeds. The hard timber is sometimes used as an ebony substitute.'

We had roses round the perimeter and a pathway on the right side. There was symmetry between our house and next door's. Both had giant bay windows downstairs and up. Parallel to the cobbled street were the backs of houses facing Wigan Road where the big park was. At the front, beyond the laburnum tree, across Osborne Road, was the Flower Park.

There was a chemist and two doctors in Market Street, a baker's and a butcher's where we went on Saturdays, two junior schools, a grammar school and a comprehensive and the shoe shop where my mum worked her first job before she became a nurse. It was a small town sown with housing developments from different eras. They were separated by parks. There was no river. All the water was in the baptismal pool beneath the floorboards in front of the pulpit in the Baptist Church.

We attended Bryn Baptist on Wednesdays and Sundays. We wrapped ourselves in hymns and were lost amongst the flock. It's where our friends and family were. And we prayed. We prayed at breakfast. We prayed at lunch. We prayed at dinner. We prayed before sleep and in the mornings. There was good and bad in the world. There was God and the Devil around us. There was darkness and light, daytime and night, black and white.

On the surface Ashton-in-Makerfield was a plain-speaking Lancashire town. Even the street names were plain-speaking: Liverpool Road led to Liverpool, Wigan Road to Wigan, Bryn Road to Bryn. Market Street is where the market was. And the road to hell went to hell. And racing through the fields, hidden from view, was the fast, furious East Lancs Road linking Manchester to Liverpool.

Ashton was adventureland – shop doors rang when they opened, milkmen whistled from milk floats, old men tipped their flat caps, a horse and cart drove through the mist early on Saturday morning. It was the rag and bone man shouting 'Rag and Bone' in three notes like church bells.

16

<u>Norman Sissay</u>   29th May, 1968.

Norman is a healthy contented child, who is well settled in this home. The foster parents are devoted to him as are also their respective families. He is a very affectionate child with a happy smiling face and large appealing eyes. Needless to say when he is taken out he attracts a great deal of attention.

Norman is well settled in his routine. He goes to bed between 6.0. and 6.30. in the evening and sleeps through until 8.0. o'clock the followin morning. He has an excellent appetite, enjoys his food. The child experiences the occasional tummy upset, but this usually occurs when he gets too warm. The day I visited, there had been a change in the weather and Norman had been upset by it, but had quickly recovered from it. He was enjoying a bottle before going to bed.

Norman is very well and appears to be very happy at the present time. He is a contented child with a winsome smile, and huge liquid eyes, which at once attract people him. He is very little trouble, and is contented both during the day and during the night. Mrs. Greenwood is pregnant and is expecting a baby at the end of August or beginning of September, but she does not seem to find Norman any trouble at all. She tucks him under her arm as nurses often do, and carries him about that way. She says she does not feel the strain. Arrangements have been made for her mother to come and stay at her home and look after Norman when she goes into Hospital to have her baby. Mrs. Greenwood's mother, Mrs. Munroe is herself one of our approved foster mothers, and we know that when this happens, Norman will be in excellent hands.

He is making normal progress for a child of his age, and as I said at the beginning, is a very happy little boy.

B. A. Oolat.
Child Care Officer.

15th October, 1968.

Norman was sitting in his High Chair when I visited today. He seems to be growing and developing into a sturdy little lad. He is very good with the new baby, and can say "My baby". He has got over his initial jealousy which was in itself very slight. He is a very affectionate child, and likes to go up to the pram and say ah! and stroke, but when Mrs. Greenwood wasn't looking, or at least when Norman thought she wasn't looking, he often tried to nip or smack Christopher the new baby, however, he has quickly got over this, and is very loving towards him. The difficulty now is, he wants to pile all his toys on top of the baby in the pram.

17

Mrs. Greenwood is an excellent little mother, and does not seemed to be experiencing any difficulty in looking after the new baby and a toddler. Norman certainly isn't being neglected because of the advent of the new baby.

In the end of September, the family went up to the North of Scotland taking the children with them. Norman, I understand caused quite a sensation, and naturally loved all the attention that he was given.

He keeps in good health and is extremely well cared for.

Child Care Officer.

14th November, 1968.

When I visited today, Norman was sitting entralled on his potty. Mrs. Greenwood is having some difficulty in trying to get him toilet trained. He doesn't take to this idea at all, and usually nothing happens when he is sitting on it, but he wets himself almost as soon as his trousers are put on. Just to demonstrate for me, how good he was, he immediately got up and placed the yellow plastic potty on his head and danced for me. This child certainly has a sense of rhythmn and he was aware that he was causing great amusement. As, has been noted right from the beginning, this child loves to get attention. He is keeping fit and well and is developing into a very fine little boy. He has got a strong will of his own, but still he does not say very much, except Mummy and Daddy, and my baby. However, he knows everything that is being said to him, and one of his favourite words which he most certainly puts into action is 'No' if he doesn't want to do something. I feel that this child will have to be guided rather than made to do things.

Christopher, the Greenwoods' first-born child, my little brother, came along in July 1968. We were opposites. He was blue-eyed, albinoish timidity and I was a brown-eyed, Afro-haired potty-on-my-head kind of child. Sarah was born two years after Christopher and eight years later came Helen.

In an effort to demonstrate how she treats the children alike, Mrs. Greenwood calls them 'toads' 'worms' 'snakes' etc. If she uses one of these words to describe Norman, she will immediately say the same thing about Christopher.

Only fourteen months apart in age, Christopher and I fought like brothers – cats and dogs had nothing on us. I adored him.

> The child is making good progress and plays extremely well with Christopher his foster brother, he is a very affectionate child, who needs to be shown that he is loved and wanted. Norman is very caring towards Sarah the baby, he no longer introduces her as my baby but stands by her pram, and with great dignity says 'this is my sister'.
>
> A few days before the family moved from their old home. Norman had come in from playing with his friends very distressed, because they had started to call him chocolate boy!.

When it came to the colour of my skin my parents referred to me as chocolate. It would have been impossible to ignore the dark-skinned heroes in 1970. Muhammad Ali was at his most famous that year. No one told me I was the same colour as him. No one told me I was the same colour as Martin Luther King. In my parents' eyes, though, there were no black heroes. In their world, Africa was full of poor people waiting to be saved.

Racist comments from the outer world became more frequent. Mum and Dad's response was to tell me to ignore it or to say back, 'We are colour blind,' or 'We are all human beings. We are all God's Children,' or else: 'Sticks and stones will break my bones but names will never hurt me.' But names weren't the problem. The underlying unkindness was the problem. We don't fear the snakebite. We fear the venom. It has been formulated inside the snake from the moment it was born. It was the underlying unkindness of other children that bothered me because it came from their parents.

My mum fostered a child as her mother did before her;

19

only my mum fostered a 'coloured' baby in 1967, in a time of racial intolerance in England. Some smiled and stopped to look at me in my pram and others spat on the back of her coat as she walked by. Years later they would do the same to me. So whatever this racism was, it would be the shadow to the light of my parents' love.

CHAPTER 3

Meet me by the morning
On the corner of night
Where the mist rises
Where love might

Every street has its weird family. Often they are not weird at all, just bohemian, childless, pious, snobby, too well educated, super-stylish. They're just different. You never think it's your family, though. No one does. Our family loved God and God loved us. We feared God. We lived in love and in fear of God. It was a lot for me to take on board, especially as I also loved Jubblys, Curly Wurlys, R. White's Lemonade, a quarter of Bon Bons, Sherbet Dip Dabs, Milky Bars. And I didn't fear any of them.

I was a happy child, always listening to adults, to what was being said, trying to pick up the root of the conversation. I was inquisitive and unafraid. Another way of looking at it might be that I was so afraid of missing something that I had to know everything that was going on around me.

Granddad Munro made wooden chests for each of us. One for Norman. One for Christopher. One for Sarah. Outside we ran free. The Flower Park, the Big Park and the copse near the school – these were my adventure playgrounds. I was a regular candidate for the early-bed brigade and spent much of my time mooning at my friends from the bedroom window.

Mum called me in one day, but for once I wasn't in trouble. Mum and Dad were in the kitchen. 'Get upstairs!' she shouted at me. But I didn't go upstairs – not all the way. I stopped to listen as she continued with the same tone to my dad.

'Just go out and do it. Now! Before the whole town sees it,' she said, banging cutlery, rearranging chairs, slamming cupboards.

Mum was a nurse. I wondered whether she was like this in the hospital when she delivered the babies. 'Just go, now! Here, take this, and you'll need a bucket too, won't you?' The sarcastic tone hung in the air.

As Dad walked out the front with a mop and a bucket, I followed. On the red-brick gable-end wall of our semi-detached, someone had scrawled in giant letters: 'BASTILLE'.

'Dad, what's Bastille?'

Unusually for him, he didn't explain, but carried on sponging the wall and said, 'Look it up.' So I headed back in for the encyclopaedia.

'Bastille was a fortress in Paris. For most of its history it was used as a State Prison . . .' The rest of the day we spent on tenterhooks. It had got to Mum. And Dad too. He just shut himself up in the front room for hours. I didn't think it had anything to do with me.

'I bet it's those kids,' Mum said.

Our mantelpiece was inhabited imperiously by Wedgwood figurines: maidens with long necks and flapping ducks on their way to market. There was a disparaging tone towards the next-door neighbours because they didn't go to church. They couldn't afford Wedgwood. And they spent their money on bingo – gambling is the Devil's work, after all. The grass grew wildly in their garden and their children were scruffier. But I liked them. I liked my neighbours and I liked their children. I liked everybody. Why wouldn't I?

Mum had short black hair and dark eyes. She had stern teeth with a slight overhang. She was the louder personality. When she and Dad argued, she'd smash plates, throw ladles. I'd sit on the stairs listening to the chaotic cacophony, the clatter that underlay the stress of relationships and parenthood. She was volcanic and volatile. I never ever imagined that the arguments might have been about me.

She smelled like mums smell; there must be a smell a child is attuned to from being a baby, a cross between baby powder and witch hazel. I don't believe that an adopted baby gets any less love from their parents than a child naturally born to them. For ages, until the end came, no matter how volatile the day had been, I would pray that she'd open the bedroom door before I slept. I'd pray that she'd sit on the edge of my bed and sing me to sleep as she did when I was younger: 'You are my sunshine, my only sun-shine, you make me happy when skies are grey . . .' I believed her.

Her smile seemed like it was fighting back sadness or tears. Dad was broody, tall, witty and silent. In contrast to Mum's agitated discordance, Dad did dad things quietly. He read the paper and occasionally let it all out on the squash court. One of the social workers wrote that he was 'basically shy and at ease talking about academic matters but more difficult when talking of personal matters'.

```
Mrs. Greenwood looked more tense and anxious and talked
abbut her job and husband's new jobrather a lot.  Husband
not too good about putting himself forward so is thinking
he may have taken on too much by becoming Head of Junior school.
He is basically, a shy person.  One has to work very hard to
draw him into discussions;  he seems alright when discussing
at an academic level but isn't really too good when trying to
communicate at a feeling level.
Told Mrs. Greenwood that we had no intention of removing Norman.
This promoted further discussion on the management of him but it
was obvious that things would not change overnight.  She accepted
this as being so but it was threatening to her to think that she
and her husband with their expertise may have gone "wrong"
somewhere!!!
Obviously need to support this couple through their unverbalised
anxieties.
Norman continues to thrive; on the whole a satisfactory placement
for him.
```

The front room was his library. It was the quiet room, which doubled up as a posh room for visitors. The bay window looked out to the laburnum tree, which at night threw gruesome shadows back at us.

Cornerstone books for me back then were the Bible and books on the books of the Bible, the Famous Five series, Secret Seven, of course, and *The Lion, the Witch and the Wardrobe*. C.S. Lewis was a rock star in our house. All of the books stacked along the bookshelf in the front room waited for our hungry eyes. I don't remember other novels or poetry – except T.S. Eliot's *Old Possum's Book of Practical Cats*, which was my favourite, and I memorised it.

Mum and Dad said I was like Macavity. It felt affectionate then, but later I realised something wasn't right. Macavity was dark, quick and a thief. Macavity was such a contrast to my blond blue-eyed brother Chris. His affectionate nickname was Bunty.

11.12.74

There are no problems with Norman. Mrs. Greenwood does not think of the boy as a foster child. He has been with this family since he was a couple of months old and Mrs. Greenwood considers him as theirs. The foster parents have spoken of adoption but they are afraid that investigations may lead to his mother.

Norman is learning to play the piano and he said to be an exceptionally bright boy. He is very much aware of his colour and often asks why he could not have been born to a white lady. He has asked if he will have to marry a "black lady". Mr. & Mrs. Greenwood are very proud of Norman and expect a lot of him academically in the future.

11 December 1974

I was a questioner. In the Baptist Church, our church, we were taught to question *why*. The answer was often 'Because we are sinners'. At school I was subject to all kinds of questions about my race, which I couldn't answer. I brought all these questions home.

'She left you . . . she didn't want you . . . if I find her I will scratch her eyes out . . . how could she . . . ?' My mum's love was elevated by how much she hated my birth mother for leaving me. That's all I knew. All I knew was that my birth mother, the woman who had my face and my blood, was from Africa and Africa was where poor people were.

25

April 1974

I'm seven.

Mr & Mrs Green wood, realize that there will be many problems ahead with
Norman, as well as a lot of happiness.   Sometimes he gets very emotional
about his colour, and when this happens he can be very aggressive.   Norman
is not usually agressive he shouts but he does not fight.

Mr & Mrs Greenwood have come to terms with the fact that his personality
is very different from their own and that of their children, he is naturally
an extrovert, happy when he has an admiring crowd round him.   He thrives
on praise and affection, in fact he can not do without it, this is part of
his heritage, and the Greenwoods acknowledge this.   Norman has asked
several times recently whether he is adopted, they have answered him
honestly that he is not, they do not think he really understands   what
it means but that it is just something that he has heard talked about at
school.   This child has a very real need to belong.   Mr & Mrs Greenwood
get very concerned about Norman's future, the only family he has known is
theirs, and he loves them, and is loved very deeply in return.

CHAPTER 4

Raise me with sunrise
Bathe me in light
Wash all the shadows
That fell from the night

I developed a sense that there was something wrong with me around the time I began attending junior school. R.L. Hughes Infants was my first school. It was straight up at the top of Osborne Road. We'd normally walk with Mum when she could take us but later I reached the age when I could walk on my own with my brother.

I liked the exact curvature of the earth of the school grounds. The green, green grass went on for ever. And the football field and running track. The neat 1960s buildings. I preferred it to home; there was less static in the air.

Mr Graves was the headmaster. He entered the hall each morning and stood near the monkey bars with his arms behind his back. They said he was an officer in the army. The music teacher sat in front of the piano. Mr Graves gave a solemn nod. And the pianist would begin with the prelude while peering over her glasses and then we would sing the song we also sang occasionally at church:

> All things bright and beautiful,
> all creatures great and small.
> All things wise and wonderful,
> the Lord God made them all.

I looked at my headteacher in awe.

After the school holidays, Christopher will be starting at the same school and it will be interesting to see what happens because Norman does not like Christopher to be better at him at anything so this could possible spurt him on to effort or on the other hand he may give up if he feels that Christopher is beating him.

I hadn't realised at any point that none of what I have told you so far is true. I wasn't a happy child. I was a deceitful one. I was causing problems for everyone. It must be true. These are the words of Mr Graves from the social worker's report of January 1976.

Spoke to Mr. Graves several times on the phone and eventually visited the school.

. He felt that Norman's successes in were too many for Chris to cope with. Went on to talk about another placement for Norman - without any consideration of how the boy might feel. I put it to him that it was the only home the boy had known,

I told him that another placement was out of thequestion and went on to inform him of what I had discussed with the foster-parents themselves. We talked about specific incidents in the school when Norman's behaviour had been inappropriately rewarded.

He is never going to learn to cope with disapproval if approval
is all he is being exposed to. The boy is going to meet with
negative attitudes being unreasonably displayed to him at some
time or other and one wonders how he will cope with this when
he is entirely unused to it.
Spoke to Norman's class-teacher. It was obvious that the boy
had a very special place in this school - staff, domestic staff
give him preferential treatment. Norman has to experience more
realistic handling and attitudes towards him have to undergo a
change but not reject him.
Headmaster will keep in touch about both children.

Visit to foster home Norman seen.

I loved life. I was nine. My brother Christopher was eight. I
loved school. I loved him. I showed my love for him by
punching him. We had the same rivalry most brothers have.
We fought with unbridled determination, the way brothers
do. We wrestled. We sweated until one of us, invariably
Christopher, would burst into tears. Catherine and David had
no children when they took me. Christopher was their first-
born but I was their first. I was the eldest. I loved my town.
I loved my family. I loved the sibling rivalry. I loved the
Market, the Flower Park, the Big Park, the books. The church.
My friends.

The headteacher suggesting to the social worker that I be
moved for the sake of Christopher couldn't have happened
in isolation – 'Norman's successes were too many'. How could
a child's successes be too many? The social worker said,
'Norman doesn't like Christopher beating him.' Of course he
doesn't. *He's my brother.* Something was at play. Something I
didn't understand. 'Norman's behaviour had been inappropriately rewarded. He is never going to learn to cope with

disapproval if approval is all he is being exposed to.' This inclines me to think my foster parents must have spoken to the headteacher prior to his speaking with the social worker, as there is no counter-narrative in the files.

All I can tell you is what my parents told me: my mum was a nurse, my dad a teacher. And my brother and sister were my brother and sister. This was our town. But I couldn't help giving my brother a Chinese burn 'cause that's what brothers do. Isn't it?

CHAPTER 5

Smouldering embers
In the sky above
Anger is an expression
In search of love

28.7.75   I called to see Norman today, the family just having returned from their
holiday in Scotland. Mrs. Greenwood was upset, it seems just this morning
Norman repeated what he had been ~~saying~~ doing most mornings while on holiday
He is getting up in the early hours and eating sweet foods, particularly
biscuits, he has eaten as many as two packets. Norman says he is sorry for
his behaviour but cannot promise not to do it again.

Eight years old. For the record, I did steal biscuits but not two whole packs. This exaggeration would come back to haunt me. What I did was this: I stole biscuits from the biscuit tin and then rearranged them in the tin in a stacked 'roof-column system' to hide the fact I had stolen them. Genius.

One holiday in Scotland at my granddad's home the family left me in the cottage, as punishment for lying about stealing some cake. Sarah, Christopher, David and Catherine walked down the hill to Lochinver. I thought I had been locked in my room but the door was open. I sobbed my way downstairs. The rich smell of silver birchwood from the embers of the fire filled the front room. Wiping tears from my face, I saw on the table a half-cut ginger cake. The tears evaporated, replaced by butterflies in my stomach. *Maybe I can have a piece*, I thought. *If I cut it in exactly the same way as it was already cut then no one will notice I've taken a slice.* Genius. And so I did. Macavity was much cleverer than that. The cake tasted so good that I figured one more slice wouldn't do any harm at all. There were no witnesses, but then there was only one suspect. It tasted so good. So I did it again. To this day I don't know why I got into this habit of stealing biscuits and bits of cake. But I did. They told me I was devious.

The problem was that my first instinct was to say, *I didn't take the cake.* I hadn't considered that the reason they had left me in the cottage in the first place was as a punishment for stealing cake. Still, I denied that I had stolen the cake. Macavity would have had more guile *and* more style. Soon enough, after another hour in the bedroom, I realised that I had to admit to taking the cake. What I didn't realise was the significance of my transgression. The lies worried them more than the theft.

This habit of stealing cake was the crack in the dam. There was something bad in me. Something I didn't understand. 'Don't look at me with those big brown eyes' was the strange refrain my mum would shout at me. I didn't understand what she saw. If I argued that I didn't know what she saw, then would I be lying? How could I see what she and my foster father saw?

Back at home, the front room was where I was punished. Same place we 'entertained' visitors, same place the books were, same place the social worker would sit. The leather sofa was polished to perfection and smelled of Pledge. Stealing cake and lying about it was an indication that the Devil was working inside me. The front room was where I was caned.

I loved the normal stuff. The middle room, where we mostly lived and watched *The Clangers* and *Crackerjack!* on the TV. The files tell a different story, though, a story narrated by my foster parents and filtered by the social worker. Within three years it will be reported that I threatened to kill the entire family, except for baby Helen.

CHAPTER 6

As the pastor dragged the 'forgiven'
From the watery grave
They'd say 'Jesus Christ'
And he'd shout 'You are saved'

It was run by the Elders. Bryn Baptist Church, a mile from
our home and a mile from Grandma and Granddad
Munro's. Occasionally, Granddad Munro played the organ
when the regular organist was away. He was always slightly
out of sync. Mum and Dad avoided looking at each other.
My Granddad, with his missing teeth, flat cap and a twinkle
in his eye, was the best granddad in the world.

Church was full of horrific stories: burned bodies and dead
babies strewn in passageways, weeping and wailing mothers,
a story of a woman who was turned into a pillar of salt,
prostitutes and beggars, lepers and mass baby killings, people
drowned in the huge flood and Jesus stabbed with huge nails,
hung on a wooden cross, with a crown of thorns and blood

pouring down His face. Poisonings, stabbings, burnings, child murders and rape.

'Repent. Repent for your sins.'

The temperature rose with the pastor's words. Girders of green, blue and red light fell upon the rapt congregation from the stained glass.

Mum threw up her arms. '*Praise* Him.'

So I threw up mine. Was I saved by Jesus? Shadows swooped over me as clouds swiped the light away. And then it was back again. The congregation flew to the sky. Chris, my brother, was looking at me, lips pressed together in a mean line, his eyes slanting.

'You stink,' I mouthed back at him.

'Praise God, praise God,' I sang out with the congregation.

I spent twelve years kneeling and praying. It's what we did. It's all I knew.

And it was the powerful rhetoric and lyricism of the church that took me to poetry. All stories in the Bible and in church had to be interpreted; everything was symbolic and analogous. Peter had lied and then repented. We should repent for our lies. The woman turned to salt for looking back. We should not look back. Jesus died so that we could live.

I wonder now at the literalness of it all. The cross on the front room wall was made of seashells and had a likeness of Jesus hanging on it. Dad decided to take Jesus (and the glue) off the cross because 'He is risen', although the glue was harder to pick off.

There is barely any mention of religion in my files. It wasn't discussed with the social worker. In my parents' eyes he was a heathen.

We seek the attention of the world from the moment we are born. An extrovert is just an introvert trying to prove they are not.

The child has an extrovert personality and is attention-seeking. He is bright academically but unable to sustain long periods of concentration and is therefore disruptive in classroom situations. He is given quite a lot of attention because of his a) pleasant personality, b) his colour and c) he is a foster child. The foster parents own children are somewhat overshadowed by this child.

CHAPTER 7

Dawn is a wake for dusk
Light will find what it must
What will be will be and thus
Shadows speak for us

The journey to Winnock became an oft-repeated one thoughout my childhood. Dad always stayed in the car when we got there. He stayed with Sarah because Sarah was too young. Winnick was a sprawling red-brick institution set in manicured greenery. It was the picture of order and quietude covering up the secrets and lies.

Mum, me and Chris walked through the front door to an archway and after Mum signed a register we stepped into the wide tiled corridor of the Asylum. It smelled of vomit, bleach, Savlon and urine. Our footsteps were louder here and followed by a sharp echo. Haunting moans pealed into the air as we stepped onwards. A nurse appeared as if from nowhere and rushed past us. Chris was chewing his lip and getting paler and paler. He'd developed a nervous habit of sucking his upper lip, leaving it dry and chapped.

Our long journey in this other world led to a big public room, like a cove, with lots of winged armchairs with women in them. I scanned the room slowly and I noticed that none of the women were right. They were holding their heads all wrong, they were strange, dribbling creatures. Then Mum spotted one of them and stepped quietly over to her. The woman had an overhang to her mouth, wolf-like, dribbling, hair like a nest, and she was rocking backwards and forwards, a twisted arm held out like a snapped twig. There was a familiar shape to her eyes.

'This is Aunty,' Mum said. 'Say hello to your aunty.'

I pulled myself together. 'Hello, Aunty,' I said. I liked her and she liked me. I could see a twinkle in her twisted slow eye as her bent head rocked back and forward and her twisted elbow pushed out a clawed hand towards me and brushed my cheek. She couldn't speak. But her grunts were enough for me to know.

Chris twitched and managed a mumble. Mum took out a hanky and lovingly wiped drool from Aunty's mouth and chin. How long did we spend there, watching her rocking back and forth? I knew instinctively not to ask questions as we headed off.

Mum visited her twin regularly, sometimes alone, sometimes with us. My aunty had been like that 'from birth' and, as children have a sense for these things, I realised that no one mentioned her: not Grandma, her mum, or my mum, her sister.

My grandmother, Phyllis Munro, never visited her daughter with Mum and us. I wonder, does Catherine believe she took away what her sister needed? What a thought! People can be cruel to themselves. People can be cruel to each other. Was my mum born in shock that she had survived? Did she blame herself? Did her mother blame her? Was Catherine living with a constant sense that she was not good enough because she had taken the air from her sister? She would do everything to prove otherwise. She would foster a black baby and show her mother (who was a foster parent too) that she *was* good, in spite of what she had done to her sister inside her mother's womb. I honestly believe that if my mum could have changed places with her sister in the asylum then she would.

Nature may be cruel but at least it is honest. It's not the doings of the Devil or of God. My aunty hadn't done anything wrong. Her sister hadn't done anything wrong. Her mother hadn't done wrong. This was not a curse for sins. If they could all let themselves see that this *is* the beauty of nature. My mother's twin sister was beautiful. She was as beautiful as any catwalk model and her mind was as relevant as Alice Walker's. It's not my aunt who has the problem. It's my grandmother who couldn't look at her, and whose subsequent hatred of her other daughter – my mother – caused my mother's inescapable feeling that she didn't deserve to be alive. No Christmas and no birthday would rid my mother of the feeling that her twin sister had a birthday and a Christmas too.

All things bright and beautiful, all creatures great and small!

There were two other sisters, Ruth and Sue, and a brother called Alec – my uncles and aunts. I think Sue was the adopted one. Ruth's portrait hung in my grandmother's front room above the fireplace. It hurt my mother, but not because she would take anything away from Ruth. It was because my mother felt her picture would never be on the wall because it would remind her mother of her other daughter, the one we visited.

I was born into a laburnum-tree family with its beauteous bloom and poisonous seeds. I saw Grandma at least once a week, and I loved her. Maybe she did love Catherine Greenwood, the twin who survived. Maybe she loved her so much she couldn't show it. Because to show it would have made her feel she loved her daughter in the asylum less. Maybe Catherine was her favourite, the one she fought for, the one who survived; she was the first. But Catherine never felt it and consequently found love difficult to give.

Grandma Munro was always cutting her down to size. The disappointment inside Mum deepened and I guess it explained her begrudging discontentment with others. The parent and daughter reinforced each other's dysfunctional behaviour like rutting stags caught in each other's antlers. In fact, all they wanted of each other was love. This was the great rift. Catherine was the first daughter and Phyllis was the first mother. And the other daughter was in an asylum. This is how anger is stoked. Bitterness rots the vessel that carries it.

None of this is in the files. Grandma was a registered foster carer with the local council, like her daughter. I never saw any other foster children there. The only time I knew of a foster child being at her house was when I was sent there. Duncan

Munro, Granddad, was an outpost, an ex-whisky-drinking, motorbike-riding maverick from Lochinver in the Highlands.

We holidayed there at every opportunity. He owned a picturesque cottage surrounded by hazelnut trees and silver birch that bowed down the hillside to the bay of Lochinver. My memories of those times are idyllic: the smell of wet heather and bracken, the majestic vision of Suilven in all its glory. If God lived anywhere it would be here, I reckoned.

Before settling down with Grandma, Granddad would often get mad drunk in Lochinver and jump on his motorbike and ride up the treacherous cliff edges like a hurricane. And now and again, I'd catch glimpses of that wild Highlander. The cottage had a little stream (a burn) that we used to bathe in. And we'd go down to the bay with him to get salmon, trout and mussels. I've loved mussels ever since.

He was a rugged, left-wing free spirit, and he'd ended up in Bryn, of all places, and there was something about me being 'other' and him being 'other' that gently brought us together amongst the nodding tomato plants of his greenhouse. I liked nothing more than standing there, clearing away weeds while he clipped the tomatoes and told me stories.

From seven to twelve Mum would send me to stay alone at my grandparents' home in Bryn. Grandma made me mop the floors, polish the furniture, sweep the yard. I can't remember any of my brothers and sisters being sent away. It's only at the time of writing that I realise it was just me. I didn't mind. I enjoyed chores.

My grandma was so overweight it would eventually kill her. She ruled over my mother with a rapier tongue and a cynical withering look, which could reduce Mum to tears. Grandma Munro was the queen of the chessboard. She surveyed the world like its aim was to take her out. There wasn't space for grey areas in Grandma Munro or self-reflection. There was a pathological need to be right about things. There was little time for reflection. There was good and bad, right and wrong, heaven and hell. All of this clarity would belie the murkiness.

I can still hear the emptiness of the school song mocking and echoing down the corridors of the asylum.

> All things bright and beautiful,
> all creatures great and small.
> All things wise and wonderful,
> the Lord God made them all.

Was there something cruel in this family, a strong undercurrent threatening to drag me out into the wide ocean? Was there something about this family that locks its damaged children into places they can't be seen and then punishes itself for the guilt it feels?

CHAPTER 8

Shadows plunder me
Beneath the sun and moon
The undercurrent under me
The electric bathroom

When my hands touched the tap, electricity surged through my body. It terrified me. I stood, naked in the bathtub, and screamed. Dad rushed in. Dad tried the tap with his hands. Nothing happened. Mum walked pensively into the bathroom. He asked me to do it again. I did and electricity shot through me. Again I screamed. Mum was standing behind him. 'Again,' she said. Dad tried it again. Nothing. And nodded that I should do it again. I pleaded with them and saw the disbelief. If they were thinking that my reaction was false, what were they thinking about me? I slowly drew both my hands to both taps. It happened again, electricity twisting my insides. It felt as if a layer of skin was being pulled from my body in the way a tablecloth can be pulled from a polished table. My mother looked more and more horrified. And this time she nodded for me to put my hands on the cold and hot taps.

Once again, Dad tried the taps. Nothing.

'Grab one tap,' she said.

By now I was crying, but they were both looking at me as if I was possessed. My dad nodded to me. My hands clasped the taps again. And again, my arms, fingers and teeth were pummelled by the electric current. I look at my mother and her face was full of disgust and dismay as if to say, 'What is inside you?'. I thought, *What have I done?*

'The water! He's in the water!' My dad was a schoolteacher. He lifted me out of the water and hugged me to him, tighter and tighter. 'He's in the water,' he said.

This memory was so clear in my mind that I thought it must not have been a memory at all.

This is how it was reported in my files:

29.9.75 | Visit to foster home <u>Norman seen.</u>

The home was in a chaotic state and Mrs. Greenwood very distressed. On Sunday the electric wiring had faulted and the bath was live when the children were bathing. Mr. Greenwood, Sarah and Norman were at risk and the two children received electric shocks. No medical attention was required. Consequently the whole wiring system was being checked over and workmen were in the house.
Mrs. Greenwood seems much given to over-dramatisation and quite held on to all the attention with her description of the events. Also Norman had a black-eye, the result of playing football last week and this too, was described in graphic detail by Mrs. Greenwood. I suspected that she was anxious in any case about my visit and focus on the family's current misadventures was a way of deflecting more direct discussion of Norman and their role.

I was nine. All the information in the reports was first curated by my foster mother and then presented to the social worker. In the report Sarah, my sister, is in the bath with me. But she wasn't. We did bath together but not this time. Not in my memory. So why would they say she was?

I was alone with the electrocution. Little misinformations in the report make invisible people appear to prove that it didn't happen *just* to me. The black eye also mentioned in the report was another little misdirection. The black eye was from being beaten up by racists. My quick mouth could outplay any racists but not my fists. And it was simply a matter of numbers.

CHAPTER 9

Look what was sown by the stars
At night across the fields
I am not defined by scars
But by the incredible ability to heal

Mum was a state registered nurse. She took a professional interest in our pain. At the hint of a scratch, a graze, a bruise, a bump, a cut or an itch she'd sit me down at the kitchen table and draw the medical kit from the top of the kitchen cabinet. Out came the witch hazel, the bandages, the scissors the plasters, the Savlon, the gauze, the medical tape and the smelling salts. I loved it. I am not sure I ever felt as close to her than when she'd say, 'This is going to hurt,' before dabbing my grazed knee with a pinch of cotton wool soaked in witch hazel.

It's because she was a nurse that she had the comb. Each morning before school I'd stand by the heater in the kitchen. The comb was a strip of metal with barely visible slits. I stood facing away from her and she stood behind. Mum dragged the comb through the roots until my skull felt like it had been dipped in acid and was pouring with blood.

'You have hair sore,' she'd say. Apparently 'hair sore' was a medical 'condition' that made the hair sore when it was ripped through with a thin comb. It felt as if the skin was being ripped from my skull. Tell a child you're his parent for ever and he will believe you. Tell a child he has hair sore and he will believe you. I believed her. I had 'hair sore'.

Then, on a spring day, Mum got me up in my best shirt and trousers. I was going to meet a pop star. Errol Brown was the lead singer of Hot Chocolate. They had a massive hit with 'You Sexy Thing'. Mum took me to an apartment in Winstanley. I remember there were bowls of nuts and crisps and it wasn't even Christmas. Errol Brown chatted to me about school and stuff. He was black like me. I was very subdued, slightly nervous and intrigued all at the same time. And then, he left the room and came back with a present for me. I stared at the strange and elegant genius of design and style: an Afro comb. 'Your very first Afro comb,' said Errol Brown.

He had been visiting a newborn child of a family friend at the hospital. Mum was the midwife on call and I guess they must have got talking about me. Maybe she showed him the thin-toothed comb she'd used. Maybe he winced behind a smile and gritted his teeth to stop himself saying, 'What in hell's name do you think you are doing with this boy? Huh? You think asking me about the comb after eight years of tearing out his hair is okay? How come you are only deciding to find an Afro comb now? Why now? His hair is Ethiopian hair! Ethiopian hair is VERY particular! Just like your hair is very particular. Why did you not get this boy an Afro comb from the day he had hair? Why not?'

He didn't say those words but any Caribbean or African (especially a parent) would question the unnecessary violence of 'hair sore'.

CHAPTER 10

Secrets are the stones
That sink the boat
Take them out, look at them
Throw them out and float

19 April 1978

There is a letter on file from Normans mother, written in 1968, requesting that he be returned to her in Etheopia - perhaps Norman should be made aware of this? — NOT YET I THINK.

The Greenwoods are ∧Normans∧ parents, and they and their natural children meets his needs in every way, their attitudes, love and concern are ever present, however, there are times when either they or Norman require Social work support and if this is requested then the demand should be met.

Jean Jones, Social Worker.

SEEN BY   AS HIS

N J.B
4/10/79

Why would the social worker, Jean Jones, say that my mum and dad 'are seen by Norman as his parents'? They told me they were my parents for ever. Why would I

53

think anything else? But why would she make the comment now? In two months' time they would send me away for ever as if I were a stranger.

As with most brothers close in age, Christopher and I fought like snakes on each other's territory. Christopher always, even in the midst of thrills, betrayed a fretfulness, as if the edges of his world were beginning to shake and his mum could see it. He was an introvert. I had no idea that Mum thought it was my fault. We raced each other home from school every day, and every day I beat him.

I waited in the kitchen by my mum. He dived into Mum's arms and said, 'Mum, I beat Norman, didn't I?' She stroked his head and said, 'Yes, you did.' And then she looked at me. 'Yes, you did.'

Over the past few years I had begun to sense that I had done something wrong and yet didn't know what it was. There were times when Dad was charged with punishing me in the front room with the cane. He asked me to yelp so that it sounded like I was being punished. Other weird things started to happen.

I was ten, and we were off to a wedding in our new clothes. Chris, Sarah and I were on top of the world. Sarah looked pretty as a picture in her blue floral dress and flower basket. Just before leaving the house, Mum looked at me for a second; something pinched her features. She said, 'Take them off and give them to him.' I didn't understand. I took off my trousers and gave them to my brother. These moments stuck in my memory. It was the sense of an underlying unkindness that stayed with me.

CHAPTER 11

How Darkness runs
From melting shade
How bright the sun
How unafraid

1973
I have only two school reports from my infant and junior
schools, which tell me something about who I was.

Character and temperament:
Norman is a carefree and happy child and, with the common
sense he shows, he is an asset to the class. His lively personality makes him popular with the other children with whom
he works and plays well. He gets on very well with his
younger brother and often seeks him out in the playground.

At eight years old in 1975 the social worker scoffs at any idea
of my having educational aspirations.

<u>Norman</u> - is a bright, responsive, extrovert child, apparently
enjoying good relationships with others. One feels however, that his
colour and foster child status draws more attention to him. He is
under quite a lot of pressure to achieve academically. The possibility
of University was mentioned and Oxford specifically quoted. Grandiose
ideas of Public School - Local Authority paying fees for Manchester
Grammar!! Norman physically fit.
A situation which, for the moment, is satisfying Norman's needs for
attention and he seems reasonably secure despite warning signals of
some emotional deprivation. It is perhaps true to say that he meets
the foster parents needs too and should he not meet their expectations
more conflict will ensue.

7 September 1976

Name. NORMAN SISSY, 2, OSBORNE ROAD, ASHTON   Case No.

Date	REMARKS
7.9.76 - continued -	There have been difficulties because of his colour - his peer group have been calling him names and swearing at him. Consequently, he has been wishing he was white!! Mrs. Greenwood has been hearing that Norman swears when out at play and says that he uses 'bad language' in the house sometimes. However, Norman excuses himself by saying that it is part of the "scene." If he does not use it when the other children do he will be thought of as 'soft'. It is important to Norman that he should not be seen as 'soft'. Talked briefly to the boy about his worth - either white or black. His comment was that being white would not suit him!!
	On the whole, fairly settled period with Norman's 'normal' behaviour being commented upon because of his colour.

To put it simply, my social worker and my foster parents considered that the school commenting on my 'normal' behaviour
was purely down to my race. I should explain this. My mother
told me that I got undue positive attention because of my
colour. This comment on my 'normal' behaviour was seen as
undue positive attention. It was a no-win situation because I
clearly got undue negative attention because of my colour. What

they wouldn't see is that I got positive attention because I was a positive child and I got negative attention because of racism.

7 July 1978
The social worker, foster parents and I were wondering which upper school I would attend.

7.7.78

Message to phone Mrs Greenwood - telephoned from home on 10.6.78.

The problem had been the selection of school for Norman - it had been accepted by Norman and the family that Ashton Grammar would be the first choice - in the knowledge that it will be comprehensive. However, Norman has been having a rough time with his peer group most of whom are already pupils of the Grammar School, and this caused the family to think again, as Norman himself did not seem happy at the prospect of going there. Also at a recent parents evening, the maths teacher had suggested that Norman was not a GCE candidate in maths, - Discussed the problem at length, and in my opinion at some future date both Norman and the family would have regretted not having giving the opportunity of a grammar school stream. Such comments from teachers tell more about the teachers than the pupils. Both the Greenwoods and Norman had eventually decided on putting the Grammar school as first choice. The reason being Norman had discovered that several of his class mates had also made it their first choice.

It was agreed that I should see Norman in school on Wednesday morning, he was aware of the fact that I had been consulted.

11 July 1978
Junior school report in full. Eleven years old.

Child's general progress:
Norman is an enthusiastic worker. Unfortunately he lacks the concentration to follow through his ideas.

Conduct:
He is co-operative and eager to please.

Character and temperament:
A cheerful happy boy.

Relationships with staff:
Very popular and extremely sociable. Norman is amenable to discipline.

Participation in school activities:
He has an amenable approach to all school activities but lacks perseverance.

Cleanliness:
Always clean and tidy.

General progress:
Norman is a most likeable boy – a ray of sunshine.

12 July 1978
The social worker's response to the headteacher:

Discussed Norman with Miss Jones, who has quite a pathetic attitude towards the child, purely based on his colour - see recent school report where she refers to him as a Ray of Sunshine $\frac{3}{6}$- she sees his colour as his cross to bear - hopefully the staff attitude in his new school will be more realistic.

CHAPTER 12

Leave alone the heartless
The landlords of decay
Light breaches darkness
Every single day

December 1978
The social worker reports that 'Mrs Greenwood had a daughter'. Her name was Helen. It was an unexpected pregnancy. The household now had four children and two adults.

Between November 1978 and the following report there are no visits and two phone calls from the social worker. This is partly due to the social worker's illness in January and February. The next phone call is on 13 May 1979 – eight days before my twelfth birthday.

The more Mum tried to beat me, the more I would run to
her for a hug. I was sent to live with my grandma for a month
and returned on 16 June 1979.

Home was now hell. I couldn't do anything right. The better I
did, the worse I was treated. I was deceitful. I was tricking
everyone into thinking I was a good kid. For the life of me I
didn't understand. A Danish filmmaker – Katrine Riis Kjær –
captures the exact confusion I felt in the dinner scene of her

documentary about the international adoption industry called *Mercy Mercy*. In this scene, two adoptive Danish parents examine their adopted child at the dinner table. She is in trouble. She looks confused. The adoptive mother speaks to the father under her breath: 'You keep an eye on her. You have to keep an eye on her.' She can clearly hear it. The young Ethiopian girl does not know what is happening. It gets worse for her. They ask her questions when her mouth is full and berate her for not answering. It gets worse. Much worse. The scene encapsulates what it feels like to be hounded by the people you have been trained to love.

16 June 1979

16.6.79

> Visit – some ten minutes with Norman on his own, the interview interrupted by a visiting Aunt. The incident had clearly shaken Norma and he felt some insecurity as to his position in the home – he admitted to difficulties of controlling his temper but insisted that he had not meant what he had said. He did recognise that his Mum was under some strain at the moment, although he wasn't sure why, told him some of the reasons, and his response was if only I had realised and he felt even more unhappy at having allowed the incident to develop.

I didn't threaten to murder the family. I have no history of threatening to murder people. Full disclosure: I probably said to my brother, 'I'm going to kill you.' Brothers say things like that in the heat of the moment. But I don't believe that my eight-year-old sister said, 'Mum, Norman has threatened to kill the whole family. Except Helen.' I was twelve! And I had just started at high school. Jean Jones, the social worker, disappears. The following report is from 2 November 1979, days before they would send me away for ever.

```
2.11.79    Phone call from Mrs. Greenwood requesting a visit.

           LATER. Home visit. Mrs. Greenwood was just returning from work. She
           told me that they had been to a parents evening at school last night,
           and that there had been very unfavourable reports about Norman.

                                                         . She says Norman
           is a naughty boy, and that she sometimes thinks he is 'amoral'. She
           told me that he smokes, swears, steals, and he seems to harbour a grudge
           about being black.

           She said she was at the end of her tether with Norman and felt she and
           her husband had given him so much, which Norman just seemed to resent.
           She said she had given him all she could and could do no more, and he would
           have to be taken somewhere where they could get to the bottom of all his
           'anti' - feelings. She said she would have him for weekends but he would
           have to go.
```

The only report from my high school is from the summer of 1979. The reports for children in care were different. This was called a 'periodic school report for child in care'. Here is the report in full:

Child's general progress:
Good progress within his form.

Conduct:
Well-behaved in lessons.

Character and temperament:
Pleasant.

Relationships with staff and other children:
Always keen to please and has many friends.

Participation in school activities:
Always willing to participate.

Cleanliness and tidiness:

Very good.

General progress:

Good progress. Noman has settled down well in his first year at this school.

Signature of headteacher:

Keith Allen

.12.79

Phone call from Mrs. Greenwood. Norman has spent a fortnight at her mothers to give her a break, and on Saturday he lied to them. He said he was not in detention, but then it transpired that he should have been in detention on Saturday morning. Mrs. Greenwood said she had had a talk with Miss Hesketh at Byrchall High, and Norman was to be referred to the child psychiatrist. Apparently while Norman was at her mothers he refused to wear his school uniform and insisted on wearing red socks. Mrs. Greenwood sees this as examples of "his unsocial behaviour". She says she knows Norman smokes and wonders where he gets the money from.

I asked why he'd gone to her mothers, and Mrs. Greenwood said that the other children go to stay sometimes.

I felt like I'd done everything to show them that I loved them, and I'd done everything to show God that I loved Him. I still had to ask God for forgiveness. And they were still my parents for ever, right? I was still her only sunshine.

On 1 December 1979 the report records that Mum called the social worker to take me away.

1.12.79

Spoke to foster parents on telephone. Both almost insisted that Norman had to leave today. Explained that we should discuss this, apart from the problems involved of getting a place. Arranged to see them on the 2nd January, 1980 with a provisional place in Woodfield arranged.

Norman Mills, my new social worker, has since told me that he informed my foster parents that having made a commitment to me as their parents it was not right for them to demand I be taken away. So I didn't go.

Mum had said time and time again, 'You are defying us deliberately because you know there's somewhere you can go: to children's homes.' She said it so many times that I couldn't deny that I didn't know about them. But even though I knew there was somewhere to go I didn't want to go anywhere. They were my mum and dad. This was my family. They had said they were my mum and dad for ever. I couldn't imagine anywhere else. How could I? So when she said to my uncles and aunts, 'He knows he can go somewhere. He uses it against us,' I couldn't deny it.

There are two sure-fire ways you can have a child put into care. You can say this kid might come to harm if he is not taken away or you can say the child might do harm to others if he is not taken away.

CHAPTER 13

He lost touch at night
Their fingertips withdrew
Nobody touched him, light,
Except you

It was the end of December 1979 and I was excited when I entered the front room for the family meeting. I was excited because the family meeting was just me and Mum and Dad. Just me. No brothers and sisters. I felt important. I sat at the table and my mum looked at me intensely.

'You don't love us, do you?'

I said, 'Yeees, I do love you.'

'We want you to spend the next day thinking about love and what it is. Read the scriptures and give us your most honest and truthful answer tomorrow.'

That was it! It was a clear instruction from Mum and Dad. I studied the question for a day and a night, I prayed to God, and I read the Bible to see if a passage would answer the question. It was a question to which I already had the answer. Of course I loved them. Mum had always said that love was never in question. I started thinking all over again.

If they were asking me whether I loved them or not, and if they were the ones who taught me about love, then maybe I didn't love them, otherwise they wouldn't ask. This led me to the answer I thought they wanted me to get to. They wanted me to ask God for forgiveness and through Him I would learn to love them. His love would shine through me to them. And in the Baptist faith a sinner must ask forgiveness for his sins. The theology was perfect, the timing unquestionable, and the answer as honest as a sinner could get.

The next day came and I said it with pride because I thought I had found the answer they wanted me to find. 'I musn't love you,' I said. I looked at their faces to see if I had said the right thing. 'But I will ask God for forgiveness . . . and *learn* to love you.' This was the perfect answer. *Seek and ye shall find.* This is what they wanted me to seek. And this is what I had found. I had found the answer.

She looked at me as if I had wounded her. 'You don't love us? You don't want to be with us?'

All of this happened the day after they had made this call to the social worker.

31.12.79   Message left after Christmas saying that the Greenwoods wanted Norman removed without further discussion.

66

Date	REMARKS	Initials
1.12.79	Spoke to foster parents on telephone. Both almost insisted that Norman had to leave today. Explained that we should discuss this, apart from the problems involved of getting a place. Arranged to see them on the 2nd January, 1980 with a provisional place in Woodfield arranged.	
2.1.80 ENTERED	Discussion at the foster home with both F.P's and Norman. Unfortunately other members of the family were also in the house, which didnt help a complicated situation. Norman was himself insistent that he wanted to leave & . A long discussion but attitudes seemed hardened and therefore I arranged to take Norman to Woodfields. On the journey, Norman spoke of 1) being hit with abelt by Mr Greenwood for smoking 2) being sent to bed at 7.30 p.m. 3) receiving little pocket money , 4) Not being allowed to attend Youth Clubs, pictures etc, even the youth club at his school.	

WOODFIELDS

CHAPTER 14

Night can't drive out night
Only the light above
Fear can't drive out fear
Only love

3 January 1980: a month after the ten-year anniversary of the 'Notice Hereby Given' sent to an address in Ethiopia by Wigan Social Services.

My mum wouldn't hug me as I left, so I hugged her. Norman Mills, my new social worker, waited at the gate. He ushered me gently into the car. I looked back but they were already turning to go indoors, mindful of the neighbours. The car filled with a quiet loss. Mum told me they would never visit me because it was my choice to leave them because I didn't love them.

We passed the butcher's and the chemist's and Wigan Road and passed the Flower Park and the main park and then we drove close to my first girlfriend's place – whenever I am that side of town I always hope I'll see Diane. We drove past the junior school, past Byrchall High School, and then unfamiliar territory unfolded before me. The East Lancashire Road: one dual carriageway, with a single destination.

This was the beginning of the end of open arms and warm hugs. This was the beginning of empty Christmas time and hollow birthdays. This was the beginning of not being touched. I'm twelve. And it is my fault. This is what I have chosen. The journey took about forty-five minutes, or forty-five seconds. Or forty-five years.

I said to Norman Mills in the car, 'I know this is my fault and I will ask God for forgiveness.'

Mr. & Mrs. Greenwood had no family of their own when Lemn was first placed with them at the age of 7 months. They have since had 3 children of their own, the eldest child, Christopher being born when Lemn was about 1 year old. Lemn remained with the Greenwood Family until January, 1980, when he moved to Woodfields Children's home, at the age of 12½ years. He has therefore never known any other family life, and to all intents and purpose still sees himself as a member of the Greenwood family (albeit a rather distant member these days), despite the breakdown of this fostering placement.

Relationships between Lemn and his foster parents had been strained for a long time although basically it was felt that Lemn derived a fair degree of security in the foster home. However, Lemn's reaction to, and non-acceptance of Mr. & Mrs. Greenwood's rather rigid christian beliefs, appeared eventually to directly lead to the breakdown of this situation. As the boy moved into adolescence, he had begun to question his lack of freedom, relative to his peer group, which had not been well received by the foster parents. Mr. & Mrs. Greenwood showed a great deal of inflexibility and lack of tolerance, in being unable to accept Lemn's rebellion against their Christian beliefs.

Lemn had tended also not to apply himself in the local Secondary School, which had not been acceptable to the foster parents either. They had long held high expectations of Lemn academically, and had seen his lack of effort, and general clowning in school as a reflection upon them personally.

Finally, the Greenwoods demanded that Lemn be removed, although they largely retionalised any feelings of guilt that they may have experienced, by pointing out that Lemn himself wanted to leave.

He kept his eyes on the road but his hands gripped tighter on the wheel. He tapped the indicator and pulled quietly into a layby and turned the engine off. 'None, none of this is your fault. None of it.' I had no idea what he meant. He must have been mad. It was my fault. If it wasn't my fault why could I never return home?

The roads started to shrink. We travelled through Lowton, through Leigh onto Orchard Lane by the pond crowned with bullrushes. 'It's called Lucky Hollow,' said Norman, but I was looking at the mansions set far from the road on the other side. Orchard Lane was broken up and potholed. The car growled and Norman and I jolted from side to side. I put my hands on the dashboard and looked up at the giant trees as we turned into the driveway of Woodfields Children's Home. Chrysanthemum bushes clambered on either side beneath sycamores and beech trees. I saw a dirty-faced boy through the bushes staring at the car then darting away. This was The Other World. This was the outside world that Mum had said I desperately wanted. I didn't.

We carried on around the front of the building to a fan of steps sweeping up to the door facing a huge garden. It was 3 January. Most of the children were away with their families. All was silent.

The smell hit me first. It was the smell of Winnick. I stood in the hallway, with my back against the wall. Norman Mills disappeared with a man into an office. I listened to muffled noises from the giant house. This was an adventure for the Famous Five.

My twelve-year-old self stood still between two doors in the hall. One led to what looked like a playroom. I sneaked a look. Sniffed once. Sniffed twice. Further down the hall to my left, a thin corridor made its way to a kitchen and the dining room and the back door and the cellar door beneath the stairs. To the right were the front door and the tiled porch. Two feet in front of me lay the clenched fists of the grand staircase's bannisters, bigger than I'd ever seen. My heart wanted to jump out of my chest and run away back to the Greenwoods so that I could tell them all about it.

I didn't lean on the wall. My arms were by my side. My shoulders back. I stood like I'd been taught a good boy should stand. Hands out of pockets. Best behaviour. I looked left. I looked right. To make a good impression I would shake hands and say, 'How do you do?' I practised, 'How do you do? How do *you* do? How *do* you do?'

I'd practised it at home with my foster dad in the front room. The posh room. Then I'd go to church and do just as I was taught. I looked left and right again. And then I smiled a big 'hello' smile. Nobody there. Just a practice. It felt good so I did it again.

Mum said it was deceitful. But it wasn't. I held it as long as I could and it felt good. I got a feeling in my tummy when I did it. Butterflies. Then I asked myself whether I could hold my breath and hold my smile at the same time. I tried until there was no air in me. Then I asked myself if I could hold my breath, hold my smile *and* think of something really, really sad at the same time but keep smiling. There was nothing sad to think about. Not really. *Okay,* I said to myself, *think of something that's always there and then imagine it's not. Got it. Right, 1– 2 – deep breath – 3.*

I smiled, held my breath and then thought, *Mum and Dad are never coming back; no one is coming back; you've lost everyone. Everyone! It's your fault.* Hold the smile. I held my breath. Held the smile. *Your fault.* I held my breath. Held the smile. Shoulders back. *Your fault.* Held the smile. Held my breath. My eyes widened till they were about to pop. I watched the second hand on the clock. *Hold hold hold.* I was a boy in a hallway, smiling, who looked like he was screaming. With a gasp I sucked in as much air as I could to replace what had left my body.

This is what I know. The world is split in two. Good and bad. Bad is evil and good is godly. I had been bad in the eyes of good. I took biscuits from the tin then lied about it. I stayed out late and made up reasons for staying out. Lying again. I had fights with my brother. And that is why I was there. I stole biscuits. I stayed out later than I should. I fought with my brother. I made people laugh when they shouldn't. I was mischievous. I had the Devil inside me. I was 'amoral'. I was devious. My parents are good and I must have hurt them. But they are not gone. They wouldn't leave me here. This is like when I went to my grandma's. This is The Outside World. This must be like a break. It must be.

A boy appeared from nowhere as my body regained composure. He'd been a gecko on the ceiling all the time. He was shuddering with excitement. 'So who da-da-da-da-da are *you*, da-da-da fucking hell.'

He fired questions at me, none of which I could answer. 'Whoareyouwhereyoubloodyfrom . . . dadadadaadadadada.'

His name was Jack. He seemed younger.

'Hello, I'm Norman,' I said and stuck out my hand for him to shake. 'How do you do?'

I know how to hold my knife and fork. I keep my elbows off the table. I say please and thank you. It's not me being devious. It is what I have been trained to do. Jack stared at my outstretched hand as if I were an alien. He craned his head to the side with a quizzical, bemused and excited look. He raised both hands to the right and left then grabbed and twisted my ears screaming 'Brrrrrrrrrrrrrrragggh' and ran off, whooping with laughter.

I was still reeling when I heard the steps of adults. Norman Mills was with Mr John Harding, a beer-bellied, cigar-smoking Manchester City supporter. He ran Woodfields Children's Home. Mr John Harding was the boss. He had fifteen staff working for him: cleaners, gardeners, laundresses and residential social workers. In those days children's homes were employment bureaus for the local community.

Mr Harding had a harsh Gorton accent. He was barrel-chested and always looked as if you might be hiding something, or as if he might be hiding something.

He showed me the dining room, and the kitchen was like a more menacing version of *Alice in Wonderland*. I had drunk a shrinking potion. The cook looked at him and switched on the industrial potato peeler. It filled the kitchen with the rumble of thunder. The steel teapot was twice the size of my head. The cupboards were full of cups. I'd never seen so many in one house.

The cellar was daunting. The low ceiling was lined with flickering striplights. It smelt of damp stone. 'It's where the servants worked and lived in Victorian times,' he said. There was a room just a little bigger than the table-tennis table that squeezed into it. Then the laundry room with industrial steam presses for the bed sheets, and a long walkway with benches, and under the benches, rows and rows of shoes.

There'd be many times in future that I would play table tennis with myself by pushing the table against the wall. Backhand and forehand smash, defend and attack, spin, cut, lob and slice. My body would skip around the table like a sprite on the solid stone floor. I would narrate the game against Christopher, my invisible brother, and I'd let him win.

Mum and Dad must have told everyone in my family to stay away from me. I hadn't realised then that none of them would contact me ever again for the rest of my life. My grandparents, aunts and uncles and cousins. Mum and Dad must have gone back to the family and said, 'We cannot contact him. He has left us. He chose to leave us. After everything we gave him.'

Whenever I got a call to leave the table-tennis table in the middle of a game against my invisible brother I'd say, 'I'll play you later, Chris. Okay?'

All my personal belongings were to go in the locker by the bed. I asked when my clothes and toys would be arriving. They were in the trunk back at home, the one with my name on it, the one Granddad Munro made. But nothing was coming here from there. Not even a Bible. I had nothing to put in the locker by my bed in the dormitory.

Over the next few weeks the children's home filled up with teenagers. Most children in care have someone they can call family. I had no one.

CHAPTER 15

Meet me by the morning
On the corner of night
Where mist rises
And hope's in sight

Peter Libbey was my first friend. He was half Chinese, half English. He was a year older than me, and his sister, Michelle, was a year older than him. 'Libbey' took one look at me, and with a big open smile he pronounced in a broad Leigh accent, 'Right. Chalky White. That's you. Chalky.' And from then on 'Chalky White' – that stereotypically lazy, drug-taking West Indian character created by a popular white TV comedian at the time – was my nickname. Every boy wants a nickname. I loved it!

Libbey introduced me to the new world. He wasn't necessarily the hardest guy or the angriest guy in the home, but he was the funniest. And he was a rugby player. Rugby was the number one sport in Leigh. We'd often go to Kirkhall Lane to watch the game. Libbey was highly intelligent, like the Artful

Dodger. He was a survivor and a grafter. He worked hard to make people like him. By calling me 'Chalky – my mate', he was shoring up against what he knew would be a tirade of unbridled racism. He was getting me to stand up to the inevitable. If I couldn't take a joke I would be in for a rough ride. Libbey was giving out a message to everyone not to mess with Chalky 'cause he's Libbey's mate and he's all right. I'll never be able to thank him enough for what lay beneath this christening. Eventually I came to hate the nickname but I can see now what Libbey was doing. And I appreciate it.

He showed me all the creaks in the upstairs landing. He taught me how to walk across it at night without a sound. His sister, was in the girls' bedrooms and they'd sit up all night chatting. There were three huge boys' dormitories on one side of the landing and the same for the girls on the other. Between four and seven of us per bedroom. I hardly slept for the first month. The sheets were stiff and forbidding. The blankets were scratchy. The base was just slats of hard wood. The mattresses were thin. The first thing the staff taught me was how to make hospital corners. These were checked by the staff every morning and if they were not done right the sheets were ripped off the bed.

Any one of us could *disappear* at any minute. We pressed our faces to the windows whenever a car arrived. *Who's next? Who's disappearing next?* We were the children of the film *La Cité des Enfants Perdus* (The City of Lost Children). Within a week I got the picture. The children's home was a holding pen.

It was a matter of days before I saw the first explosion. It happened in the dining room. There were about twenty of us in Woodfields. A tall, quiet boy called Red stood up, He flipped the dining table onto its back and kicked his chair against the wall. Mr Harding burst into the room, grabbed him and wrestled him to the floor. Red fought back but it was impossible to fight against Mr Harding's trained technique. A report would be written about Red. There would be consequences. He would disappear. We knew. We all knew that this place wasn't interested in our trauma. The institution wanted us to shuffle through the days and nights, fulfilling the rotas and jobs with no trouble, and then disappear. I had to pretend that I was okay and hope that my smile would last.

4.1.80	Saw Norman at Woodfields. He seems quite happy at present, obviously enjoying the 'comparative' freedom by way of contrast to the foster home.
ENTERED	He is insistent that he wants to remain at Byrchall H.S in Ashton and I have said that I will contact the school after the weekend when it officially reopens. I am aware that the Greenwoods do not want Norman to continue at the school, as they feel that he will cause problems for their son Christopher.
8.1.80	Spoke to Mr. Allen, Head of Byrchall H.S.
	but does not feel that he should continue there.
	Have explained this to Mr Harding, Woodfields and have arranged to visit Burchall to see Deputy Head Miss Hesketh.
14.1.80	Visited Byrchall and spoke to Miss Hesketh. She felt that Norman has caused some minor problems in school i.e. not doing his homework selling his dinner tickets etc, but otherwise no serious difficulties. However, Norman had not done well academically- generally preferring to fool around. Miss H did feel that Norman had been allowed to attend the school disco/Youth Club.

N. Mills. S. Social Worker. NM .

<table>
<tr><td>18·1·80
ENTERED</td><td>Visited Norman at Woodfields. Very unhappy about the Birchall decision, and none too happy about the prospect of attending Leigh CE Secy. Resentful of the F.P's and schools. attitutde , but still wanting to see the Greenwood & family a.s.a.p. Norman however embarrassed about going home. I therefore to make arrangements with the Greenwoods for Saturday 26.1.80 and to go with him. Norman could then make his own way to Leigh or Greenwoods could take him by car. Norman more agreeable to this offer.</td></tr>
</table>

N. Mills S.Social Worker. Nh .

Norman Mills, my social worker, didn't understand that my foster parents had no intention of taking me back. I didn't understand it either. I couldn't imagine that I'd never be able to return. My social worker had no idea they had indoctrinated me into believing that I had evil inside me and that the evil had chosen to leave them. So I fought the 'evil' without knowing what it was and ran away – to them – to say please help me. I had no one else to run away to.

A foster child will expose the cracks in the familial veneer. Insomuch as the foster child is a cipher to the dysfunction of a family and also a seer. But the responsibility is too great for a child and so he finds himself manipulated and blamed for what he exposes by the simple virtue of innocence. The wrath this innocence incurs is deep and dark.

My foster parents said they were my parents for ever. They taught me to say 'Mummy' and 'Daddy'. They trained me. They said they were mine for ever because my birth mother didn't want me. They were my mum and dad. The reason I am writing this book is so that they can get a clear idea of what happened. They stole the memory of me from me. The only sense I received from them was the sense that I should disappear.

The second of May 1980 was nineteen days before my birthday.

21.5.80	Normans 13th Birthday today.
	N. Mills S Social Worker.
5.6.80	Visited Woodfields and saw Norman who was in a much more affable mood than when I last visited him. He did not receive any cards from the Greenwoods on the day of his birthday- but fortunately these arrived next day- containing a £5 note. This seems to have pleased Norman a great deal.
	Recently I had contacted Mr and Mrs Greenwood when we learned that Mrs G's father had died.of whom Norman was very fond. Had asked the foster parents if they would like to convey this news to Norman personally.- but ultimately they did not do so and the staff at Woodfields told Norman the news. Norman has taken the news well.
	We had an interesting discussion today re Ethiopia and Normans Mother which Norman obviously enjoyed and I feel was useful to him. He is displaying less resistance to the idea of being fostered out again, but wary of another breakdown. He states that he wouldnt want to go to a coloured foster family.
	School is still not a happy place for Norman but he blames this on his own attitude. He has been punched and kicked today by a lad from Woodfields but didnt seem to be resentful towards the other boy. Physically, he has no serious injuries. He has apparently been much happier of late, according to the staff and is looking forward to going to a holiday camp this month with the C.H.

21 May 1980

My first birthday in the children's home. No one called.

CHAPTER 16

I work in rain said the storm
Thunder broke his heart
I woke in light said dawn
And spun the sun in the dark

I quickly learned my place with rotas and bells and wake-up time and supper time and shoe-shine time and teatime and hospital corners and kitchen duties. My life became a set of systems and my existence was defined by how well I performed them. No love. When I cheekily challenged the staff about why they chose this as their career they would say, 'I do this job because I love children.' In all my time in the children's home they never said, 'I'm in this job because I love *you*.' I was becoming invisible. I had been in Woodfields for eleven months.

12 December 1980

Visited and saw Norman today. Norman in rather a truculent mood
when I spoke to him about glue sniffing. He insists that a number of
the other lads at Woodfields are also glue sniffing, which I was
already aware of. However, I emphasised the dangers to his health
and appealed to his intelligence.

Norman spoke quite freely of his recent association with Mr. & Mrs.
Greenwood. He had initially visited with Christmas presents for
the whole family, and the relationship with the Greenwoods had then
appeared to blossom again, to the extent that the Greenwood's had
stated that Norman's behaviour was 'much improved'(The foster
parent's had then suggested the possibility of Norman returning to
live with them, according to Norman (although they have not contacted
myself or Woodfields to suggest such a move). However, Norman realises
that he is only acceptable to this family if he behaves in a certain
fashion, as the perfectly behaved foster child, and that he could not
keep up the pretence for any length of time, and nor would he want
to do so.

Norman attempts appears to be able to see the superficiality of his
relationship with the Greenwoods, and I feel that it is a very healthy
development, for this young lad to have decided for himself, that
he does not wish to return to the family permanently. However,
he has also decided that he does not want to spend Christmas with
them either, which is perfectly acceptable to the staff at Woodfields.
The Woodfield's staff and I are supporting him in this decision which
obviously is not all that easy for Norman to make, and has undoubtedly
placed him under great emotional pressure.

44

When the giant triangle rang out for dinner the house sprang
to life. Kids raced downstairs from the bedrooms, upstairs
from the cellar, swooped down the bannister, dived inside from
the garden, through the back door, through the front door,
through the cellar windows, off the roof and through the fire
escape, off the trees, every which way to the dining room.
Someone crashed into the back of me, deliberately, in the
hallway. It was Danny – arms too long, legs too long, bad skin,
bad teeth. I turned around, indignant. He looked at me as if
to say, *What?*

Two hours after dinner was suppertime. Hot chocolate and a biscuit. There were two suppers for different ages. After supper we watched TV in our pyjamas and then to bed and lights out.

Christmas Eve, 1980

My social worker sees what the Greenwoods are doing to me, and the superficiality. If they kept their hands by their sides they hoped that I would realise that I was hugging them but they were not hugging me. I wasn't going to ask my social worker if I could visit them for Christmas. I wanted them to ask me not to be alone on Christmas Day. So I did what they wanted. I stayed away. As impossible as it was to understand I grasped the idea that I wasn't welcome. I was not welcome.

The unfortunate side effect of all this however, is that Norman is now refusing to consider any move to another foster home basically because he feels that he cannot face the possibility of another Foster Home breakdown or rejection. However, given time, these attitudes may hopefully change. Norman is also refusing to speak to a local Leigh Reporter concerning her series of articles on children in care (which Mr. Ellis had suggested Norman for). SW

Visited Woodfields with a present for Norman, but did not see him, because all the children were attending a pantomime. The staff have bought him a watch for Christmas, along with other items, and everyone is looking forward to a pleasant Christmas. No further contact by Norman towards the Greenwood's and they have never contacted him at Woodfields since he came into care. 24.12.80

N. MILLS. Senior Social Worker

Children from homes all over the North West were taken to Blackpool in a convoy of black cabs and Rotary coaches to see Lancashire legends and national heroes Cannon and

Ball that summer. Lenny Henry was their special guest star. Mid-performance Lenny did a bit of what's called 'crowd surfing'. With his open and smiling face he said, 'I need one of you on stage.' He theatrically cast his eye from left to right with his hand shielding the light as if for a better look. A Mexican wave of hands flew into the air: *me me me me me!* But all the children in our group screamed at Lenny and pointed at me: *him him him him him!*

Memories in care are slippery because there's no one to recall them with as the years pass. In a few months I would be in a different home with a different set of people who had no idea of *this* moment. How could it matter if no one recalls it? Given that staff don't take photographs it was impossible to take something away as a memory. This is how you become invisible. It isn't the lack of photographs that erodes the memory. It is the underlying unkindnesses, which make you feel as though you don't matter enough. This is how to quietly deplete the sense of self-worth deep inside a child's psyche. This is how a child becomes hidden in plain sight. Family is just a set of memories disputed, resolved or recalled between one group of people over a lifetime, isn't it? And if there is no one to care enough to dispute, resolve or recall the memory, then did it happen? I had to check with Wikipedia to see if Lenny Henry ever even played Blackpool. It's there. It's right there in Wikipedia.

'*You!* What's your name?' Lenny Henry was talking to me. I couldn't reply because the others were shouting '*Norman. Noooorman*'.

'Right then, Norman, come up here then,' he said, and so

I got out of my seat, walked down the aisle and up the steps. Up until that point I was nervous, but on the stage I was unafraid. I was home. The stage lights only made me shine. Look at this man. He's black like me. And he's a star. My first time on a professional stage was with Lenny Henry. And I can't remember any more than that.

Of that particular season in Blackpool he has since said via Wikipedia, 'the summer season was the first time I felt that my act had received a proper response from an audience'.

Same for me. And I loved it.

CHAPTER 17

We are wildfire
Wild as the wind
Wild as the dawn
Wild within

Cigarettes were important in Woodfields. I learned fast. If someone goes for a smoke the first person to shout 'save us' gets the last few drags. I was at the most potent stage of a life-shortening lifelong addiction but the staff didn't care enough to tell us not to smoke. They provided us with a smoking area outside. I was twelve. If the adults don't care that a twelve-year-old boy is smoking, why should he care? In the same way, if the adults don't care to hug a child, why should he feel huggable?. What are the repercussions for a child who isn't hugged? I was becoming untouchable. We all were. The law of the untouched was unspoken.

No wonder some young people harmed others. Danny had it in for me from the beginning but he was biding his time. I worked out how to insult. Pretend you can't see them. Freeze them out. It was a powerful weapon for me because everyone liked Chalky. So I used it on Danny. I cut him out. I talked through him or around him as if he wasn't there. No one could cause me more pain than I felt inside. I was unafraid. Unafraid of bullies. Unafraid of being hurt.

Like all attacks it happened both superhumanly fast and eerily slow. In the bedroom Danny ripped the front of a cabinet from its dovetail joints. I knew it was for me. I put out my arm as he hit me with it, hard and fast in blunt, ugly disorientating whacks. No one tried to stop him. Between each smash I asked, 'Are you done yet?' I went silent. Only his grunts preceded each smash. He carried on until he was tired.

The next day Danny told me I reminded him of his brother and his brother wound him up. We shook hands and it was forgotten between us. He was hurt by the reminder of who he loved, and the love he missed. Hurt people hurt people.

In plain English this was his way of saying I am the cock of this place. 'The Cock' meant the hardest, the strongest. But we both knew that fists were not what we needed to survive here. We were already beaten.

Days later I saw Danny pinned to the floor with his arm twisted behind his shoulder. One of the supervisors had his knee on Danny's lower back. Who knows why? I could hear him whimpering, pain shooting through his shoulder as the supervisor pushed his wrist further up saying, 'You like that, d'ya? You want some more of that, d'ya? You want to take me on, d'ya'? Danny was making strangled panicked breathing sounds. He couldn't speak. He looked at me and closed his eyes. This place was wrong.

Children were moved haphazardly from home to home as objects of low emotional currency. Damaged goods. It was nothing personal. You had to have your wits about you to hold on to anything. Money, lighters, socks, bracelets, biros, cigarettes, all of it needed secure hiding places: under floorboards, holes in brickwork under a windowsill. The frequent changing of such hidey-holes kept us all busy.

By now I was famous at my school and in my area. I was Chalky White. Up for a laugh. But it was all shielding an onslaught of daily racism. Not a day passed without 'nigger' or 'coon' or 'wog' or 'black bastard' firing from someone's lips into my face. I had to be alert to punches and kicks from strangers or phlegm flying across the classroom or pavement. I was permanently in fight-or-flight mode. My main weapon was my smile, my guile and my ability to run.

But I loved the daily walk from Orchard Lane to Leigh C. of E. High School with our gang from Woodfields, down potholed Mill Lane, passing the nodding horses in the low mist of Marshes Farm. I was Chalky White from the moment I arrived. Libbey was in the year above. I loved school because I could smell family on the other young people. I could sense their mums and dads by their packed lunches, their new football kits and even by the way they talked.

I was in Woodfields for a year but it felt like ten. Shaking hands on my 'green' arrival, becoming Chalky White, skating on Lucky Hollow in winter could all have been idyllic. Mr

Marsh from Marshes Farm off Old Hall Lane employed us boys. We baled hay throughout the summer holidays and stacked the hay in his barn. I acclimatised to the disappearance of my family and to the fact that any one of us in Woodfields could disappear at any minute. Regardless, I held on to the idea that my foster parents would come for me one day. But in truth I was letting the idea go. The last hug I'd had from an adult was the stuttered one on the doorstep of their house. I had been in the children's home for 360 days. I was a world away.

CHAPTER 18

When the war of night's over
Said the wave to the bay
Let's be each other's selfie
And save the day

I wrote a poem in the dormitory on my first day at Woodfields. It was about a tree. In writing about the tree I wrote about myself. Now I can see that. I couldn't then. That is creation. In finishing a poem I felt the same sense of being that I had in church. It was a discovery, a freedom. *This is who you are.* I knew there and then that I wanted to be a poet. I had written poetry in earlier childhood but this was me and me alone, channelling something bigger than me that proved I wasn't alone. The proof was there on the paper. The evidence. I was alive.

In the children's homes the written word was rare. Letters were rare. There were no books and consequently no encouragement to read. The staff were rarely seen with a book. They were too busy adjusting rotas and shifts. There was no question of university. The suggestion of university was for more deserving people. The children's home may well have been housing us but it wasn't caring for us. The children's home needed to work with efficiency, not love. The act of writing would follow me wherever I went. No one could take it away from me.

At Leigh C. of E., my high school, I was summoned to the office of the deputy headteacher. Never a good sign. She had heard about my writing from my English teacher, Mr Unsworth. There were two lights outside the deputy head's office. Red for stay, green for enter. The red flickered out and after a pause the green blinked on. Mrs Jones had the teeth of Ken Dodd and wore jackets and trousers. '*Sit down*,' she said. I sat, sharpish. In those days, teachers smoked in their rooms and she stubbed her fag out in her ashtray and walked round the desk (the desk top was barely lower than her forehead). 'I want you to have this,' she said, and she held out a book.

It was *The Mersey Sound*, published in 1967, the year I was born. It was battered and well-thumbed, the greatest compliment to a paperback. In the first poem on the first page by the poet Adrian Henri it mentions an orphanage. All I knew about being a poet is that a poet wrote poetry. It's all I ever wanted to be. I was fourteen. This was a flag in the mountainside, a base camp.

But there were more pressing reasons to write. One boy from Leigh C. of E., who lived in a house further up Orchard Lane, asked, 'So where do you live then, Chalky?' I said, 'Woodfields, on Orchard Lane.' He looked at me quizzically at first, as if he didn't have a clue where it was, then said, 'My dad says it's a den of thieves, boy.'

It became clear to me that the adults around me had no idea what to do with me. I was surrounded by teenagers who, maybe, felt the same. The home was bedlam. I started glue sniffing with the other boys.

Visited Woodfields and saw Norman following a phone call from / 15.1.81
Woodfields staff. Spoke to Mr. & Mrs. Harding who explained that
Norman has again been in trouble. He has recently accompanied a
number of other Woodfields children in stealing a number of eggs
from the kitchens, which were then thrown at the house of a foreign
doctor nearby, in the grounds of Leigh Infirmary. In addition to
this, Norman is still suspected of glue sniffing, whilst his
attitude towards members of staff is beginning to deteriorate quite
noticeably. There are suspicions that Norman may have been involved
in other offences, which have not yet come to light.

Norman is the youngest of the youths in Woodfields, and generally
it appears that there may be a lot of pressure on him to be a
part of the group, and thus to join in the various anti-social
activities. Spoke to Norman about all this this evening, but he
was in a particularly truculent mood, and complained that he was being
singled out. However, I pointed out to him that his present behaviour
contrasted markedly with the standards he had been brought up with,
and neither I, nor the Woodfields staff, wanted to witness such a
marked deterioration in his behaviour. Norman did not agree that he
was subject to pressure from the older youths in the home to conform.

Spoke again to Mr. & Mrs. Harding after seeing Norman and it was finally
agreed that we should attempt to move him to a F.G.H.-preferably
Gregory Ave., in order to remove Norman from the influences of the
older youths in Woodfields. Norman is still antagonistic towards
being fostered, and there is therefore no point in pursuing this
particular avenue at present, as it would be doomed to failure.

It has been agreed with Mr. Roberts at D.O. and with Gregory Ave., 22.1.81
staff, that Norman can move there next week. We have therefore
arranged to move him on the 30th January, whilst I will see Norman
to inform him of the move on the 26th January.

Visited and saw Norman today at Woodfields. Norman unhappy about
the move, and protesting that he did not want to leave Woodfields.
However, I have explained to him that he will still be able
to attend Leigh C.E. nearby, and that the move is being made in his
interests, and not as a punishment. It has been agreed with
Woodfields staff that he can retain contact with Woodfields, and
can visit occasionally for tea etc. Norman appeared to be accepting
that he was moving, and did not protest to any great extent. I wonder
in fact whether he doesn't feel some relief at leaving Woodfields,
and the pressures exerted by his peer group.

SW
26.1.81

ENTER

Collected Norman from Woodfields and took him to Gregory Ave. He
already knows the staff at the F.G.H. because he has visited there
before with Peter Libby. Norman made a rather weak effort at
persuading myself, and Woodfields staff, that he still didn't want
to leave, but in fact came with me without much fuss. There was a
small party at Gregory Ave. when we arrived, and Norman obviously
felt self conscious amongst the other children at the home. He is
the oldest boy in this F.G.H. and is sharing a room with a younger
lad (Shaun). Left Norman after a time, and arranged to visit soon.

30.1.81

ENTER

GREGORY AVENUE

CHAPTER 19

Not lost said the sun
At the start of the day
Just following instinct
Just finding my way

Norman Mills reassured me that I could go back to Woodfields to see Libbey and everyone and that Libbey could visit Gregory Avenue. I hated Gregory Avenue and I hated being moved. I'd lost everybody again. The adults around me had no idea what to do with me. And that scared me. I was losing respect for them. And that scared me.

There was no time to get used to the decision, no say in it, just like the last time. No time to say goodbye. January 1981. The door opened into the 'family group home' and I felt the files closing behind me. File is an anagram of life. It was claustrophobic. The garden was tiny compared to Woodfields', and behind it, at the top of a hill, loomed a concrete hulk of a place, with a singular chimney belching out smoke: Wood End Assessment Centre.

Wood End was one of the names we passed around between us at Woodfields. The names of children's homes were my points of reference, part of my orientation into the system. The institutions: Wood End, Hindley Detention Centre, Redbank. Today I hear about these institutions in the newspapers under headings like 'Wood End Abuse Probe'.

I was well and truly part of the system. This was not extended leave. My mum and dad were not coming. It dawned on me. The whole damn thing dawned on me. The Authority was just holding me in a series of houses run by disaffected adults. I was shown to my new bedroom. I still called my foster parents Mum and Dad. I had no other terms to describe them and no one to describe them to. 'David and Catherine' sounded weird. 'Foster parents' too.

Wood End was a remand centre. Libbey told me that 'remand' is what happens when you wait for sentencing. I wanted to tell people around me, *I have no one.* Most young people in care have someone, one person at least.

Brian and Val Street ran Gregory Avenue. Honestly, I despised them and I despised the name of this place – a 'family group home'. Brian and Val lived there. The other staff lived nearby. It was homely in the way a grotto in a shopping store is Christmassy. It was false. I could see the cracks. The staff were on shifts like elves in the grotto. There was an office, like in Woodfields, from where I was passed pocket money each week, and a staff room where the staff smoked and talked about us. I was fourteen and I was confused.

Phoned Val Street, who explained that Norman is settling in, although 5.2.81
expressing resentment against being moved at ~~will~~ all .

Norman has seemed very low in spirits since his move and has been   Feb 81
refusing to do his homework or exams at school, in an attempt to
blackmail us into returning him to Woodfields. I have spoken to
Mr. Wilkinson, deputy head at Leigh C.E. and explained the situation
and also to Mr. Roberts, Residential Manager at D.O. . I do not feel that
we should give in easily to Norman's 'blackmail' attempts, as to do
so would,

1. reinforce this type of behaviour for the future and

2. would perhaps undermine Norman's security, if he felt that he
    could get his own way so easily.

Visited and saw Norman at Gregory Ave.   ____ from   30.10.81
Woodfields C.H. was at Gregory Ave. having tea with Norman,
when I arrived.

Norman in a very cheerful mood today, readily insisting that
everything was 'great' e.g. school, life at Gregory Ave., etc.
Felt that Norman was tending to put on an act and showed myself
to be somewhat sceptical. However, the lad genuinely seems to
be reasonably settled at present, and he responded more positively
to my visit on this occasion, than has been the case of late.

Initial questions, probing, from Norman concerning the possibility
of   · coming to live at Gregory Ave. Conversation then
moved on to the Greenwood family. Norman has apparently decided
that he does not now want the Greenwood's to attend his Case
Conference, although I couldn't get a clear reason why this was so.
He also informed me that he had spoken on the telephone recently
to his former foster parents and told them that he would not come
to them for Christmas. Norman did criticise the Greenwood's on
this occasion for their having failed to even contact him after
he left them in 1980, which I feel is a healthy reaction. On past
occasions Norman had tended to blame himself for this obvious
rejection, but fortunately he can now lay the blame where it should
lie,~with the Greenwood family.

I didn't want to go to my case conference because I couldn't
see it being of any use whatsoever. The case conference was
where they made decisions about me and where I sat to hear
them make judgements about me. At Christmas I got a radio

103

alarm clock. I tried it out but it didn't work. And that broke me.

When I was tucked into bed the staff wrote their reports. They had the last word on everything. My teenage self could not deal with this at all. The report seemed only to document anything untoward. My wellbeing was defined by how many marks *against* my name were in that report . . . I was three years away from leaving care. I started to ask questions about my origins. Who was my mother? Why was I in care in the first place? Where was I from? Why was I here? In realising my foster parents didn't want me I wanted to know about my birth mother. The only person who could help me was my social worker.

A fourteen-year-old boy should never have to ask the questions *Who is my mother?* and *Who are my family?* These were not easy questions to formulate in the mind or the mouth because the question comes with others . . . *What did I do to deserve this?*

CHAPTER 20

Born under mist last night
Dawn is a gift over dew
I read beneath its light
And turn over leaf to you

Gregory Avenue was in a village next to Leigh called Atherton. Athertonians were honest, hard-working salt-of-the-earth people, like the people of Leigh. They were increasingly unemployed mill workers and miners, tradesmen and retailers. In the early 1980s the Tory Prime Minister, Margaret Thatcher, set out to break the miners and the North. Thatcher waged war against the Argentines abroad, and the welfare state at home.

The mills in Hag Fold were cathedrals without congregations. And just on the edge, on the other side of Hag Fold, was Pretoria – a set of hills, the result of the second biggest mining explosion in England. In December 1910, the Pretoria Pit disaster took out 344 men and boys, a good chunk of Atherton. Women lost husbands, sons, brothers, all at once.

Pretoria now is a forest of silver birch and eerie ponds. I'd walk up there and sit atop and look across the Lancashire plain to the city of Manchester.

I spent three years in Gregory Avenue but as much time out of it as possible, like any teenager.

Gregory Avenue was on the edge of Hag Fold Housing Estate. I got to know everyone on the estate. I'd wave at a driving instructor for three years. She used our estate as her training ground. She wasn't from the estate but I was in love. She was beautiful because she always looked out for me and waved back. It became a game.

Tony Concannon lived on Devonshire Road. He ran the boxing club in Atherton and his wife worked in the taxi firm next door to it. I'd spend evenings at their house, smoking and drinking cups of tea with them and their kids. Mrs Concannon brought films back from the video shop. And so I saw all the new films before anyone else. I took whatever affection and acceptance I could from anyone who knew me.

I spent Saturdays popping into different houses on Hag Fold Estate for cups of tea and gossip. Tony had two dogs. He took them lamping up to Pretoria at night. Lamping is how you catch rabbits. The dog sees a rabbit. Tony shines a light in the rabbit's eyes, it stuns the rabbit, and then the dog pounces. Tony brought the rabbits home, I think, and made stew.

I'm still unhappy at Gregory Avenue and so my social worker suggests youth groups.

However, Norman said he was not interested in joining these groups.
Norman still telling me that he will not put in any effort in
school, but I explained that this was pointless and wouldn't
change the situation. Spoke to the staff before I left and we
agreed that it would not be in Norman's interest to transfer him
back to Woodfields, before he has had sufficient time to settle
at the F.G.H.

Have spoken to the staff at Gregory Ave., on different occasions   March 81
concerning Norman. He is gradually beginning to settle, and
appears to be making new friends in the Atherton area. He has
asked to attend an engagement party in a local pub this month,
but the staff and I have decided that he should not go, mainly
because he will be with much older teenagers and adults, and there
will be alcohol available at this party.

Phoned F.G.H. today, enquired about seeing Norman today after   26.3.81
school. I spoke to Norman who informed me that he was going out,
had something pre-arranged. He seemed much more cheerful than
recently, and in fact told me that he was beginning to settle in
Atherton. Arranged to see him next week. Mrs. Castledine at
Gregory Ave., agreed that Norman seemed more cheerful of late,
and was hardly ever in the home in the evenings.

Visited today and saw Norman. He confirmed that he has made a   3.4.81
number of friends in the locality, and now spends all of his spare
time in their company. His rebellion against moving, both in the   ENTERE
home and at school appears to be over.

Norman appears to be building up a good relationship with Brian
Street, and seems to welcome the male influence on his life. He
is particularly keen on football at present, and seems to spend
many evenings kicking a ball about, as well as attending Manchester
City's games with Peter, Libby and Mr. Harding on occasions.

Norman has had no contact with the Greenwood family since December,
and seems to put them completely out of his mind. However, he is
still feeling antagonistic towards the possibility of fostering,
and unfortunately we cannot therefore pursue this possibility yet.

Case Conference at Gregory Ave. attended by Norman (see conference   7.4.81
minutes on file). Decision for Norman to remain at F.G.H. for
indefinite period, in order to allow him to regain his sense of
security, and for no action to be taken on fostering at present.
Conference confirmed that Norman is now beginning to settle in his
new home, Mr. & Mrs. Harding from Woodfields also attended at our
request and again explained the reasons for Norman's move. Also
agreed that Norman spend Easter weekend with a local Scoutmaster
who is known to the F.G.H. staff.

Norman has requested to be allowed to stay overnight at a friends   23.4.81
house on the 25th April, friends being the Callands of _, _____ 1
' .Γ Have heard of the family previously (good reports)
and visited today to check that everything all right.

The estate had a comforting, familiar rhythm to it; the mills changed shifts at 2 p.m. and 6 p.m.; the mines had their shift times too. Payday was on Thursday for the miners, Fridays for the mills, when the pubs got lively and when stomachs were full. The shops shut for a half-day on Wednesdays. There was a Catholic Club for the Catholics and the working men's club for the Protestants. Women weren't allowed, except on Thursday nights for the whist drive. I was the boy from nowhere, from nobody, who was everybody's somebody. Chalky White.

We did discuss Norman's mother on this occasion, after Norman   SW
had raised the topic. He is very interested (naturally) in
knowing more about his parents, and how he came to be in care.
Told him again what I know of the situation, and of the difficult
position his mother must have faced, e.g. being a young unmarried
mother in a strange country. I did suggest the possibility
that we could write to mother's last known contacts in Ethiopia,
which Norman was very enthusiastic about. Also suggested possibility
of meeting people in Social Services locally who had met his mother,
but warned Norman not to build up hopes prematurely.

Drove Norman and Peter to Leigh afterwards, Norman intending to meet
his girlfriend whom he described as being 'half-caste' and a member
of a Leigh family. Before leaving however, spoke to the new
houseparent Lorraine, who explained that Norman has also recently
discussed his mother with the staff of the home. Norman is
currently enthusiastic about attending a child care course in
Newton when he leaves school, but Lorraine did suggest thatthis was
solely because Peter ‾ ′ ′ ′ and his sister Michelle were also
intending to join this course after leaving school. Lorraine confirms
that Norman is still inclined to mix with much older lads in the
Atherton area and has got himself drunk on the odd occasion.

                    N. MILLS. Senior Social Worker

                                                                        SW
                                                                        Nov/Dec 8′
Enquiries made locally through members of the International Red
Cross to see if there are possibilities of tracing Norman's mother
in Ethiopia. However, it appears that the political situation in
Ethiopia is so delicate, that the Red Cross would not become
involved in following up enquiries in that country. It has been
suggested that we try contacting International Social Work agencies.

I had been on earth for fourteen summers. And to ask me
not to 'build my hopes up' was heartbreaking, given that all
I had was hope. I needed an answer to the question, why?
Neither the social worker nor the foster parents took responsibility for what had happened to me – certainly not the blame.
The most institutionalised people in the care system are the
workers.

CHAPTER 21

What was taken I have used
To make myself a home
The stone the builder refused
Will be the head cornerstone

On my fifteenth birthday I visited the Greenwoods.

SW
16.2.82

ENTER

Saw Norman today at his Case Conference in Gregory Ave., F.G.H.
Quite a useful conference, at which it was agreed that Norman would
remain at the F.G.H. and no further action be taken concerning
fostering in the near future. Mr. Brown, Norman's Year Tutor
(also his Sport's teacher) at Leigh C.E. attended, and spoke very
positively of Norman's attitudes in school.

After the Conference, showed Norman some of his mother's details,
re her D.O.B. and residence whilst in the U.K. 15 years ago etc,
which he was seeing for the first time. Norman is naturally keen
to learn more of his mother, and we have agreed to try to arrange
for him to have contact with people who knew his mother in the
Wigan area. I discussed the possibility of my contacting Mr. & Mrs.
Greenwood for photographs of Norman as a child, but Norman resisted
this, and asked if he could be left to do this. I agreed to this
entirely, as I feel that Norman should be allowed to maintain control
with his former foster parents, but at his own pace.

I did learn today that when Norman visited the Greenwood family on Christmas Day they refused to bring him back to the F.G.H. despite the fact that there was no transport that day. Mr. Street brought Norman back on that occasion.

Visited and saw Norman today on his 15th Birthday. He was somewhat euphoric today, extremely pleased with his various birthday presents, and particularly with the various money he had been given. In all, Norman had received over £20 in birthday money, and he was keen to go into Bolton this weekend to buy himself clothes.

21.5.82

ENTER

However, Norman is more and more questioning the staff's decisions at the F.G.H., and attempts to draw me into taking sides with him against them. He went on at length to me about whether it was right that he should have to buy new shoes for himself out of his own money, stating that he had been told this by Mrs. Street.

However, when I subsequently spoke to Val Street, she explained that Norman had had a lot of clothes bought for him of late, and that at present there was insufficient money to buy him a new pair of shoes. However, if Norman was prepared to wait a little longer, the F.G.H. would buy them. Norman however, would not wait, and was therefore attempting to use me to manipulate the situation to his satisfaction. Arranged to see Norman next week, so that we could have a further conversation then.

Visited and saw Norman this evening. He was still raising the subject of the new shoes, and generally complaining that he doesn't like Mrs. Street, claiming that they can't hit it off. It is obvious that Norman is a lad who is pushing for more and more independence, but he does want his own way in so many things, and this is leading to clashes with the staff. Although Norman claims to be very happy living in the Atherton area the staff point out that he associates with much older lads, and that he has drifted on occasions recently into the home of a fairly disreputable character who lives near to the F.G.H.

28.5.82

ENT

52

When my social worker showed me the information about my mother I knew there had to be more to the story. The foster parents were determined to wipe me from their family story. Something was wrong. I figured that I could return to them to find out what really happened. It didn't go well. October 1982.

I was introduced to Bob Marley by a friend on Hag Fold
called Lyndon Marsh. I was nearly fourteen when Marley
died and Island Records were pushing out his music. Lyndon
was a huge fan. He introduced me to marijuana at the same
time.

I was spellbound by the album *Survival*. It flooded into my
bloodstream. Robert Nesta Marley loved Ethiopia. His funeral
in Jamaica was on my birthday, 21 May.

Marley shouted down the forces of oppression. In his words
I heard my own story and felt a growing pride. I am a survivor,
a black survivor.

Bob Marley was my first black mentor, my first black friend.
He spoke of suffering, history, the truth of the world and of
'Babylon'. He would be my guide. I dropped the name Chalky
White. It was no longer a joke.

What also captivated me about Bob was his way with meta-
phor and how he drew from the Bible. In a deceptively
complex song, 'Ride Natty Ride', he wails:

But the stone that the builder refuse
Shall be the head cornerstone,
And no matter what game they play,
Eh, we've got something they could never take away,

. . .

And it's the fire – FIRE – it's the fire – FIRE.

For the first time I identified myself as a black man amongst a sea of whiteness. Marley cheered me on. The more people around me denied my race by saying they were *colour blind* or that *we are all human beings* or that *we are all the same* the more I realised that race confused them.

By 1983 I had been in Gregory Avenue for two years and I was becoming what Rastafarians called 'Conscious'. It was the consciousness Marley spoke of in 'Natural Mystic'.

CHAPTER 22

Secrets are the stones
That sink the boat
Take them out look at them
Throw them out and float

I left school with few qualifications and started a Saturday job on Leigh Market. Mr Waddington was a market trader and salesman and he had a stall that sold household detergents and toiletries. I started in the early morning with a bacon butty and hot tea. I was good in the market. I liked the quick-fire humour and the work ethic of the markets. I was smoking marijuana heavily by now. In two years' time I would be leaving the care system.

The Waddingtons befriended me. I and the other boys who worked for him were cheap labour, but it was labour we appreciated. I graduated from the market stall to door-to-door deliveries.

Mr Waddington drove the Transit van crammed with tubs of bleach and detergents for floors and windows, and conditioner and shampoo, and from the Transit van I saw a bit more of the world, the reality of the 1980s industrial landscape. I handled money for the first time. Peter Libbey got me the job.

We were trusted with the products, trusted to knock on the doors, trusted with the cash. We'd feast on the estates of Lancashire, Bolton, Wigan, Rochdale. To a fifteen-year-old it was great work experience. Money in my pocket. The big wide world. Mr Waddington waited at the wheel while we ran door to door back and forth with our bottles and cash.

I worked in his warehouse too on a small industrial estate in Leigh. I had to stir the bleach concentrate into a giant vat, then pour it from a tap into the bottles and stack them up. Bleach was the abiding aroma of my youth. The vat was twice my height and equal in width. I sat atop it and stirred the concentrated bleach into water with a wooden stick. To test it I put my finger in and if it turned white it was ready. There was no breathing apparatus and no protective clothing. Mr Waddington was the embodiment of Margaret Thatcher's dream, selling cheap household products to the people who hadn't the money (any more) to buy from the shops.

When social services found out about my work, I was immediately required to pay the children's home some of my wages.

Norman's 16th Birthday.   21.5.83

Have contacted Mr. Waddington, and visited. He maintains that   JUNE 83
Norman is not working full time for him, only Saturdays and odd
days. For this he receives £10 on Saturday and 'a couple of pounds'
when he comes in the week. Mr. Waddington maintains that Norman
only comes 2 - 3 days at the most. During these days, he runs errands
or tidies up - often does nothing at all. Mr. Waddington says that
he wants to keep Norman 'off the streets'.

He is hoping to arrange a full time job for him at Bright Mills with
a friend of his, this will be a factory job, with a Mr. McGlenn.
Norman is first in line for a job apparently because of Mr. Waddingtons
influence.

Mr. Waddington said he would try to keep records of Norman's earnings,
although still states that Norman gets possibly £14 - £16 per week
off him.
                                                                           So

                                                                           SW
I understand from Mr. Lee, District Officer, (Residential Servies)   4.8.83
that agitation about Norman's right to pocket money, despite the
fact that he appears to be working part time, continues and that the
matter is likely to be raised at the 'Who Cares' meeting on Friday
next.

It appears that Norman works for a Mr. Waddington and earns £10 for
Saturdays plus £2 or £3 per day when he works during the week.
Norman is insistent on his right to pocket money in addition to this
regardless of the fact that he is unwilling to pay for his board
at Gregory Ave.

I had a long discussion with Norman on the subject and he appeared
to accept that his right to pocket money must be questionable in view
of his earnings and non payment of board. By his own admission he
is rebellious and one feels will argue the point regardless in his
present mood. When it was put to him that he would have to contribute
to his upkeep in a 'normal' family and that he may be allowed to
keep 'Saturday' earnings in that situation he mellowed a little.
However he pushed the point that he only worked in the week because
he was bored. I told him he could expect his weekday earnings to
be taken into consideration when any board or allowances was
considered. Norman said he was only asking for about £20 in lieu of
back pocket money to May 28th, 83 but by my calculation this would
be nearer half his entitlement if it were justified - Norman himself
had done a quick calculation I feel and realised that to make an offer
in settlement may be fruitful. It was also pointed out to him that
in September he would have to register unemployed to obtain benefit
and that if he was to have a correct record of contribution or credits
he would need to carefully look at his present activities and the
likelihood of a Local Authority charge on his income for his
accommodation. Norman takes these observations in a rather
disinterested way.

'Norman bought a guitar for £30 on Saturday? The source of his money.' The statement *could* have read: 'He has showed initiative in saving money through his Saturday job to buy himself a guitar' and 'It is good to see that he has saved to buy, of all things, a musical instrument.'

118

CHAPTER 23

I am not defined by darkness
Confided the night
Each dawn I am reminded
I am defined by light

During one of the trips round Bolton selling the Waddingtons' household detergents, on an estate called Daubhill the atmosphere changed. The streets were quiet. The doors were daubed with red swastikas. All of them. Swastikas. I tried knocking on a door, then a second. I could hear a baby inside. Footsteps, and then nothing. My guts churned. I told Mr Waddington about the swastikas and he said, 'Yeah, it's where Pakis live.' We were both quiet. 'No point knocking on those doors.' But I felt closer to them than I did to him.

There were riots all over England in the 1980s: Brixton, Toxteth, Bristol. The last one was in Moss Side, Manchester. The papers were full of 'rampaging youths'. Racial tensions, unemployment and routine police harassment of black people. All my life I had been told about the bad black people of the big city: the muggers and the drug dealers. A sense of barely suppressed panic took root in me because I knew it wasn't true. I was the people the people around me feared the most.

Chalky became a haunting, not a name. I needed it to stop. I needed to stop it. If it was only a joke about my colour why did people get angry when I asked them to stop? Behind the veil of the race joke was hatred. There was no one to guide me on these matters. I had my instinct. I am a black man, I said to myself. I am a black man. I am not colour blind. I am a black man. I am not Chalky White. I am not a nigger, a coon, a wog. I am a black man. I changed, seemingly overnight, from the cheeky chappy, the happy-go-lucky joker, into a threat. And it hurt me. How could identifying who I am be a threat to people?

I couldn't unsee the shopkeeper flush red from the neck upwards at the sight of me. Or the store detectives following me in the shops. At the bus stop, I couldn't unsee the woman clutch her handbag as I stood waiting for the bus. I couldn't unsee that no one would sit next to me on the bus. I couldn't unsee men glaring at me. I couldn't unsee older men leaving the pub looking at their women looking at me. I couldn't unsee people in cars craning their necks to stare at me, I couldn't unsee the people from the tops of the buses pointing at me and laughing, I couldn't unsee them hacking up phlegm and spitting at me from the bus. I couldn't unsee the police watching me or the police cars slowing down deliberately as they passed. I couldn't unsee the cars accelerating as I crossed the road.

* * *

Thatcher was taking away their jobs. She rolled hand grenades into their villages, stood back and let them explode. 'Now,' I'd hear, 'we got niggers coming in.' But I was born here. I was born amongst the mills and the mines. I was born in the villages. Overnight, I became an enemy in my own town. And I was afraid and angry. The marijuana didn't help.

I hated the home I was living in and the staff who were there. I hated the racism but I never lied to my social worker. I knew that smoking marijuana was wrong but I told him all the same.

Spent a long time talking to Norman about drugs and specifically cannabis. He denies ever having brought the drug into the F.G.H. and I warned him severely of the consequences of doing so. Also brought in Val Street and informed her of Norman's admission in his presence.

Norman's taking of cannabis is apparently linked to his embracing of the Rasta culture, which he assures me is against the use of all other drugs. I did express my strong reservations against cannabis taking. Norman doing his best to assure me that it is not harmful etc. Apart from this conversation, Norman is still expressing a great deal of resentment against Mrs. Street.

N. MILLS. S.S.W.

CHAPTER 24

Whenever I look back, said night
You're there.
Looking back is okay, said light
But don't stare.

In August 1983 Gregory Avenue Children's Home set out
for a holiday to Poole in a minibus. Maggie Thatcher was
on the radio sounding plucky. It may have been be the holidays
for the likes of us, from the children's homes of the industrial
wastelands, but the Iron Lady had work to do after her elec-
tion victory. She was rolling her sleeves up, sharpening her
knives.

On returning from holiday I decided not to wear shoes.
Poole was hot and lots of people went barefoot on the beach
and even on the streets as they made their way back to the
hotels. Why put them back on? I thought to myself. Why wear
shoes anyway, what's wrong with not wearing shoes?

Back in Atherton I stayed barefoot. Barefoot was my

rebellion. I might have subconsciously got it from the 1979 film *Scum*, about a group of boys in a detention centre. There was a barefoot guy called Archer who did it solely to inconvenience the 'screws'. That was good enough for me. It was my rebellion to the whole town and the whole system. If you want to stare at me I will give you something to stare at!

My feet were like a child's hands gripping all the different textures of the world. They were grounding me. They were tethering me to earth. My young skin cracked and split; an upturned knuckle of glass twisted into my foot and plucked the skin out like a tin opener. But I grew a harder skin: skin that could eventually walk on glass. In my files there's no reference to my bare feet. Looking back, I can see this was a desperate plea for help. Again the marijuana didn't help.

In November 1983 social services started looking into my employment with Mr Waddington and investigating his financial records – he claimed to have kept no records of what he paid me. The social services made me into a liability and Mr Waddington sacked me unceremoniously. I felt deeply betrayed. I returned to the warehouse with a Stanley knife and slashed some of the bottles of bleach.

Norman has been accused of damaging property in Mr. Waddington's warehouse, slashed some bottles and has either resigned or been sacked. Spoke to the Leigh police today, and asked to bring him to the station next week.   23.11.83

Visited Norman who informed me that he had recently walked out on Mr. Waddington, and subsequently has gone to his warehouse and slashed plastic bottles containing bleach. Wouldn't tell me exactly why he had done this, but when I suggested that he felt badly rejected by Mr. Waddington, and had reacted thus, he would not comment.   24.11.83

ENTERED

124

This introduction to the police would come back to haunt
me. They were aware of all the young men at the children's
homes. When a child runs away from the home the police are
called, so I was aware of them and they were aware of me. I
had *no* respect for the police at this time. They represented
The Authority. They were overtly racist. *Fuck the police* was my
general attitude and theirs was *fuck you.* They were out to
punish me as much as possible for less than £10 of damage.
A caution would mean I wouldn't have to go to court. But
they had triggered The Authority. Someone in The Authority
was opening my file.

I found another job within a week at a clothing factory in
Atherton. At the tail end of the era of apprentices I became
an apprentice cutter. I worked an Eastman cutter.

The factory manager thought himself a character and spent
his days nipping the bottoms of the women. The women
mainly worked on the ground floor in rows of giant sewing
machines like on *Coronation Street.* They received packages of
material from a chute on the floor above. That's where the
cutters were. Three old men with tape measures round their
necks and me.

There were three long tables, each the size of a billiard
table. Raised slightly above the table on a cylinder was a roll
of cloth. I drew the material from the cylinder across the giant

table like a bedsheet then clipped it to the end. I repeated this until the sheets of material were about an inch in depth. With chalk the shape of a shark's tooth I drew patterns onto the material using cardboard stencils. The stencils were in the shapes of the front and back of a dress, or the front and back of a pair of trousers.

The Eastman cutter was a vertical automatic saw, with a finely serrated blade. It slid beneath the fabric on the table.

'Put it on the side of the cloth, that's right, lad, and push this lever down so it grips the cloth. Now press the red button, hold tight, and push and cut around the shapes. That's the way. When you've fully cut the cloth, pull up the block of material, tie it up with a strip in bunches. Arright? Throw them down chute.'

The trousers and dresses would find themselves on market stalls throughout the North West of England and eventually they would dress the families of the North West too. Out of the blue, I received a call to the police station.

I'm not a thief and I'm not a liar. Smoking cannabis at such an early time in the development of my brain was not good. But anything that would take me away from the madness seemed reasonable. I dabbled in LSD and magic mushrooms too. Other worlds opened up inside me and I couldn't control them. Once I hallucinated without taking the LSD; it scared me enough to make me stop.

Many parents have children who have dabbled. Fortunately most young people find their way through it and, like me, they stop. But if a child in care does the same he is treated in a very different way.

Christmas was close, too close. My mental health deteriorated rapidly. I started to walk via back streets. I found main roads too intense. I didn't want to be looked at. The sewing machines at the factory were like tanks drilling into my head. The patterns on the long table became a turtle's back. A table transformed into a giant turtle and looked at me while slowly munching the old man.

The noise tormented me and I couldn't do it any more. I couldn't smile. I opened my mouth but nothing. No words. I couldn't go back to work. I could barely walk to the shops. The world started to stutter like a faulty VHS tape. The sun started to hurt my eyes. My head was falling apart and the people in the home didn't seem to know. They worked in four-hour shifts. They couldn't see what any parent would have seen in their own child – a mental breakdown.

There were five days till Christmas. Christmas was the one day in the year that I was most aware of loss. It was the one day in the year where it became obvious that I had no one. There was nowhere to hide on Christmas Day. My contempt for the adults around me was difficult to hide. One of the staff wrote a report and called my social worker, describing abusive language and aggressive behaviour, and said she wouldn't be answerable for her actions if it happened again. It was a threat but it was also a signal that I would have to be moved. Four days till Christmas. Three days until Christmas. Two days till Christmas.

I warned him that Senior members of the authority had suggested a move to Wood End, which I personally don't agree with at this stage, hoping to have Norman realise the seriousness of his attitudes. However, as I felt we were making little impact today, arranged an emergency conference for the 23.12.83, which Mr. Sumner (A.O.) agreed to chair.

SW

Conference at F.G.H. at which Mr. Sumner made Norman aware that he was on 'probation' concerning his behaviour, that he would be moved (probably to Wood End) if he stepped out of line again. Norman very truculent and negative afterwards and it wasn't possible to hold any sort of conversation with him. However, he is allowed to remain at the F.G.H. for the present.

23.12.83

ENTER

Who were these 'Senior Members of The Authority'? Couldn't they see that Gregory Avenue was virtually empty? The other children had gone home to their families for Christmas. When a child in care of The Authority comes into contact with the police 'Senior Members of The Authority' are alerted. I was on their radar. Meanwhile, my social worker had been trying to find my mother.

CHAPTER 25

Above the water
darkness greets light
Here upon the bridge
There upon the night

```
        NM/SW                                    N. Mills

                              38

    13th October, 1982

    The Secretary,
    North British Conference,
    22 Zulla Road,
    Mapperley Park,
    Nottingham.

    Dear Sir or Madam,

    I am writing to you in the hope that your Church may be able to help a teenage boy
    in the care of this Authority, to trace his natural mother's present whereabouts.

    Briefly, the facts are as follows.  In 1967, a young student named Yemershet Sissay
    arrived in Wigan from Ethiopia, where she gave birth to a son, whom she named Lemn.
    Miss Sissay was a member of the Seventh Day Adventist Church, and gave the Wigan
    Authorities as her address in Ethiopia the following:  The Ethiopian Union Mission,
    P.O. Box 145, Addis Ababa.  Miss Sissay placed her child in the care of the Wigan
    Social Services Department, and returned to Ethiopia some time in 1968.  Whilst
    in this country, Miss Sissay was a Student at Newbold College, Binfield, Near
    Bracknell, Berkshire.
```

Miss Sissay's child Lemn, was originally placed with foster parents, whom it was hoped would adopt him eventually. However, the boy was eventually rejected by this family, and has since lived in local Children's Homes, refusing to consider any further fostering placements. Lemn is now 15 years of age, has no family in this Country and is very interested in knowing more about his natural mother.

However, we have no way of even knowing if she is still alive although if she is, she would still be a comparitively young woman. I have written to you therefore because of Miss Sissay's association with your Church, and in the hope that your Church may still have ties with the Church in Ethiopia despite the traumatic happenings in that Country.

May I ask on behalf of Lemn, if this is the case, and whether or not therefore you would be able or willing to make enquiries as to Miss Sissay's present whereabouts. As the child's Social Worker, I obviously feel that he could benefit considerably from having some news, or even contact concerning his mother.

However, I appreciate that this could be extremely difficult to even attempt, and hope that you will not mind my approaching you in this manner.

Yours sincerely,

109

N. MILLS (MR.)
Senior Social Worker

130

North British Conference of the
SEVENTH-DAY ADVENTIST CHURCH

22 ZULLA ROAD, MAPPERLEY PARK, NOTTINGHAM, NG3 5BZ   Telephone: NOTTINGHAM 606312, 621965

20 October, 1982

Your ref: NM/SW

Mr N Mills
Metropolitan Borough of Wigan
Social Services Dept.
Area Office
82 High Street
Golborne, Lancs

Dear Mr Mills,

I tried to contact you this morning by 'phone, but you were not available.

I have discovered that Yemershet Sissay was a student at Newbold College at the time you indicated. She had excellent references from Ethiopia and, in fact, had been at one time the secretary to the Principal of our College in Ethiopia, a Dr Bjerken, who is now a lecturer at Newbold College.

He has suggested that you write to the President of our church in Ethiopia:

> Mr Gebre M Felema
> Ethiopian Union Mission
> P O Box 145
> Addis Ababa

You will get more information from them than you are likely to get from here.

Hoping that your search will result in something positive for the boy concerned,

Yours sincerely,

R H Surridge

131

At Christmas my social worker gave me letters copied from my files.

22nd March, 1968.

Miss Yemarshet Sissay,
c/o Newbold College,
Binfield,
near Bracknell,
Berks.

Dear Miss Sissay,

      I write to inform you that Lemn is still in my care and is accommodated in a very good foster home, with every expectation that he will settle down with his foster parents until he is able to look after himself and will enjoy their full support for as long as it is needed. He is in very good health and is a happy child.

      It has not been possible to place your baby with parents who would adopt him legally, but I am hopeful that these parents may wish to take this next step later on.

      In the meantime, I must ask you to keep in touch with me, even though you may leave the country, as your written consent will be necessary at some stage in his life.

      I should like, also, to remind you that it is my duty to assess you for a contribution towards the maintenance of the child, and I should be glad to receive your comments on this.

      I realise that you are a student but feel sure that you may be able to make a weekly payment to cover this aspect.

      With every good wish,

Yours sincerely,

Children's Officer.

132

The Children's Officer says, 'I write to inform you that Lemn is still in my care.' And yet at that time I am recorded in the files as 'Norman Sissay'. They lied to my mother. And then I read this:

C. D. Watson, President
A. A. Andreassen, Secretary-Treasurer

Yemarshet Sissay
Ethiopian Union Mission
P. O. Box 145
ADDIS ABABA

Telephone 47220
Cables :
'Adventist' Addis Abeba

Departmental Secretaries

Negassa Aga, Educational
H. Palm, L. A. & B. C. S.
G. R. Rigsby, M. D., Medical & Temperance
Bekele Heye, Sabbath School & Publishing
G. Gustavsen, Ministerial & M. V.

4th July, 1968

Your Ref. NG/AR

Mr. N. Goldthorpe, Children's Officer
Children's Department,
Civic Buildings
Parson's Walk
Wigan

Dear Mr. Goldthorpe:

You might have wondered where I disappeared. But I got a telegram telling me that I had to come home to Ethiopia because of my Father's serious illness. I came the very next day I graduated from Newbold College. With God's help I managed to pass all my examinations. When I came home I found my Daddy at Hospital and it took me quite a while to recognize my own father. He is just skin and bone. I didn't expect him to live one day but somehow he is still alive. It is just a miracle. So much about myself.

Could you please help me in answering the following questions?

1. If I want to get Lemn out here what steps should I take? I would very much like to bring him. Last week someone came came to me - that was the pilote - asked me for excuse and explained what he has done - and what has happened to me thereafter. I told him everything just because I thought it would be fair for the child otherwise I don't have any love for the child at all. I told this person as well. I told him that he is the crulest person in the world, and that I don't want to see his face at all. For Lemn's sake I have to make some arrangements with this man. Lemn needs someone to take care of him. He needs to be in his country, with his own colour, with his own people. I don't want him to face discrimination.

2. Could you give me his Foster Parent's address.

3. I would like his miSire name to be Gedday not Sissay

    Please answer me very soon. I would like to get over this problem soon. I know life is a problem, but it is good to solve the very urgent one first.

    Had it not been for your help I don't know what I would have done. I owe you very much.

    I wish God's blessings upon your rewarding work.

        Very sincerely yours,

        Yemarshet Sissay

4 July 1968

They lied to me. Someone did love me. My mother.

How can I get Lemn back? He needs to be in his country, with his own colour, his own people. I don't want him to face discrimination.

Why would she say, 'I don't want him to face discrimination,' unless she had experienced it? Why would she say, 'How can I get Lemn back?' if she didn't want me? She explains that she got a telegram telling her that she had to come back to Ethiopia because of her father's illness.

Copy of Air Mail from N. Goldthorpe to Yemarshet Sissay - 2.8.68.

Dear Miss Sissay,

I was very surprised to receive your letter, and to find that you are back once more in Ethiopia.

I realise that it would be best for your son to be amongst his own family, but I must take very great care that all would be well for him if he were sent out to you.

He is in very good hands at the present time, and is with excellent Christian folk who are doing extremely well for him.

I am afraid that I cannot give you their name and address. You will realise that this is because they may eventually adopt him, providing of course that you give your consent to this. You were adamant about this when we interviewed you, and were determined that this should happen, because you thought that this was in his very best interests.

Please give this a great deal of serious thought, and write to me again.

Yours sincerely,

Children's Officer

135

It didn't take long for my joy at receiving the letters to turn to anger. A shadow crawled into me. Nobody spoke of depression then. I found myself walking to the front door of Gregory Avenue and then turning back to my bedroom. The Authority in charge was the same Authority who wouldn't give me back to her. They had everything to hide. All I knew at the time was that I felt unsafe because the staff who were looking after me had no idea about my story. Once I received my files from The Authority their subterfuge became apparent. Everyone had been lying. The Greenwoods had lied from the start.

There is a letter on file from Normans mother, written in 1968, requesting that he be returned to her in Etheopia – perhaps Norman should be made aware of this? — NOT YET I THINK.

11.12.74

There are no problems with Norman. Mrs. Greenwood does not think of the boy as a foster child. He has been with this family since he was a couple of months old and Mrs. Greenwood considers him as theirs. The foster parents have spoken of adoption but they are afraid that investigations may lead to his mother.

My birth mother did nothing wrong. She was not poor. She was not destitute. She did not abandon me. She did nothing other than find herself pregnant while in England and ask for help.

Norman Mills gave me my birth certificate. I looked at my name, my Ethiopian name, the name my mother gave me. Lemn Sissay. *I am Lemn Sissay*, I said to myself.

I didn't know how to pronounce Lemn. I thought the 'n' in Lemn must have been a spelling mistake by a lazy registrar

136

so I pronounce it 'lem'. On my left hand are the initials NG and the nickname Chalky from when I tattooed myself in Woodfields aged fourteen. I did it with a blunt pin and Indian ink. I stabbed my hand hundreds of times and forced the ink into my skin. Bulbous, crusty scabs grew over the raw flesh. That's how you tattoo yourself. Then the scabs fall and, hey presto, there's the tattoo. After a few days though, I tried to tear them off but it was too late, the ink wouldn't flow out. Now these 'handmade' tattoos are barely visible just beneath my skin, like ghosts. At around the same time I slit my left wrist with a razor blade.

But now I knew my name. My real name was Lemn Sissay. And I knew my country. Ethiopia. I decided there and then. I would call myself by my name and I would ask anyone who knew me to call me by my name. And when they asked, 'Why have you changed your name?' I would tell them, 'I didn't change my name. This is the name on my birth certificate. This is the name I was born with. This has always been my name.'

My name is Lemn Sissay. My name is

Lemn Sissay. My name is Lemn Sissay.

My name is Lemn Sissay.

CHAPTER 26

I stand in light perfectly still
A shadow moved then hid
I've no more than what I saw
I've nothing to prove; It did

With my change of name, strange nocturnal behaviour and going barefoot, people in the town did think I was losing it. And the truth is I was losing it. The Authority seemed not to understand what was happening. Christmas passed. And I folded into myself. Norman Mills took me to the police station for a conference about the 'malicious damage' to the Waddingtons' property, which amounted to a grand total of £9.26.

Couldn't anyone see what was happening? It felt like a betrayal. Norman Mills admonished me for 'smirking' at the policeman. I had no fear of the police officer and no respect for the police. They were guarding The Authority. But the £9.26 was to have ramifications. The Director of The Authority sent this on 18 January 1984:

To Director of Social Services, Wigan: From 6 M Area Office, Tyldesley:

Ref ....   Internal Telephone No. ....

F.A.O. Residential Section   Ref .... CEW/MVR

Copy to Golborne Area Office

Copy to Gregory Avenue, F.G.H.

18th January, 1984

Re: Norman Greenwood (d.o.b. 21.5.67) ^c/o Gregory Avenue, F.G.H.

Norman was conferenced at Gregory Avenue on 17th January, 1984. I list below the Conclusions of the Conference.

1) A formal Review was postponed in December, 1983, as Norman had just started work and it was felt important not to disrupt his work pattern.

2) An emergency Conference - chaired by Mr. Sumner had taken place on the 23rd December, 1983, as Norman had displayed aggressive behaviour towards a member of staff. Norman had been given a firm warning and placed on "probation".

3) The present Review Conference was to look at the up-to-date situation.

4) The following facts were reported on 17th January, 1984.

   a) Norman has displayed further very provocative and aggressive behaviour towards Mrs. Street.

   b) He was aggressive towards younger children in the Home.

   c) Mr. Mills had taken him to be cautioned at the Leigh Police Station on the 13th January, 1984, for an offence of malicious damage to the property of his former employer. Norman had smirked at the Police Inspector during the caution.

   d) Norman is very unpredictable - can be pleasant one moment and aggressive the next.

   e) He has a "great chip on his shoulders".

   f) He has damaged a door to the kitchen cabinet at the Home.

   g) He has given up his job since the New Year.

   h) He appears to be in financial debt.

5) It was felt that Noman had not fulfilled the conditions of the Conference held on 23rd December, 1983, and that we had no option but to consider moving him.

6) We looked at the alternatives open to us. Norman is too young as yet for bed-sits and it is doubtful whether he is mature enough, in any case, to cope with such a situation. He would need an extremely tolerant lodgings landlady, if such a person exists. The ideal placing for his needs, at this point in time, would appear to be a working boys' Hostel.

7) Mr. Mills and the Residential Section were given a time limit of two weeks to investigate such a provision. Failing this it was recommended that Norman be transferred to Oaklands and if there is a considerable deterioration in his behaviour and attitudes, immediate transfer to Woodend should be considered.

I didn't give up my job at the clothing factory. Not in the way they were implying. I couldn't venture outside, therefore I was unable to do the job. I was in no more 'financial debt' than any other sixteen-year-old. The more I look at this, the angrier it makes me. The people in charge of caring for me were building a case against me because the court case had triggered the Director of Children's Services. It had little to do with me.

The reason the director was involved was because of the police charge and £9.26. But the police were called because of the accusation by Mrs Waddington. Mr Waddington sacked me, as we now know, because Social Services were making enquiries into his books.

I am unsure about the kitchen cabinet but let me confess to it. Let me say that it was me who broke a kitchen cabinet. I was a teenager. It was 1984, George Orwell's *1984*, and I was in the depths of a breakdown.

It was felt that Norman had not fulfilled the conditions of the conference held in December 1983 and that we had no option other than to consider moving him.

Mr Mills and the residential section were given two weeks to investigate the provision of a working boys' hostel. Failing this, it was recommended that I be transferred to Oaklands and if there was considerable deterioration in my behaviour and attitude, immediate transfer to Wood End should be considered.

Norman Mills desperately tried to find a place for me away from all this. He tried to get me out because he could see what was happening. I would call this institutional panic.

See Case Conference notes. Norman not happy with being moved — still extremely negative attitudes.	17.1.84
I contacted 2 voluntary organisations in the Manchester Area re possibility of taking Norman in their working boys hostels. Mrs. Cottriall at H.Q. also followed up another hostel in Stockport. Ultimately however, Senior Management have refused to agree to Norman's placement on grounds of financial cost. Therefore, Norman moved to Oakland's today. (1.2.84)	17.1.84 – 1.2.84

15th February, 1984

Mrs. J. Ogden,
Principal Child Care Officer,
Boys & Girls Welfare Society,
57A School Hill,
Cheadle,
Cheshire.
SK8 1JE

Dear Mrs. Ogden,

RE: NORMAN (LEMN) SISSAY

Thank you for your letter of the 1st February, 1984 and for the information enclosed concerning 'Highlea'. I apologise for the delay in replying to you.

Unfortunately, since passing on this information to our Residential Manager, Senior Management of this Authority have decided that they are not prepared at present to agree to finance a placement outside this Authority for Norman. Coupled with this situation however, Norman himself is currently beginning to display as being very unsettled and anxious, and a further move at this time would therefore now seem to be highly inappropriate for him anyway.

For the present therefore, we are obviously unable to proceed with an application to your Society concerning Norman. However, may I thank you for your assistance, and express the hope that we may be able to approach you again at some future date if possible.

Yours sincerely,

N. MILLS
Senior Social Worker

OAKLANDS

CHAPTER 27

I work in rain said the storm
Thunder broke his heart
I woke in light said dawn
And spun the sun in the dark

Oaklands in Lowton was a vast Victorian mansion, like Woodfields, on the opposite side of Leigh to Atherton and Gregory Avenue. If Woodfields was bedlam, Oaklands was feral, out of control. John Harding, once the head of Woodfields, was now the head of Oaklands. My anxiety and depression tightened their grip on me.

I sought solitude. And walked and walked alone at night. I couldn't stop thinking. I found an arch, over an old road, a bridge. No one could see me so I sang. I sang into the reverb of the arch. I sang Marley songs and recited my poems. I saw the houses across the fields, the orange light from the lounges and bedrooms of families and the children's home far away.

How can you be sitting there
Telling me that you care
That you care?

. . .

We're the survivors, yes: the black survivors

'Survival' – Bob Marley

The cynical attitude of John Harding at Oaklands was countered by a few staff who really did care. But I became more and more insular. More and more broken. Norman Mills warned me that Wood End had been mentioned. So I told him, I had to tell someone: *I can't go outside in daylight. I'm shutting down.* I needed him to know. I needed it recorded.

Norman has now informed me that he is suffering from certain symptoms which I would assess as being of an anxiety/phobic complaint. He is confused about his identity and no longer wants to be 'Chalky White'- everyone's favourite coloured comedien. However, he appears to have a very low self image, sees himself as being stupid, and can't talk to others freely. Says this is why he gave up his job.	13.2.84 & 18.2.84
He appears to be phobic concerning leaving the Children's Home, walks down back streets to avoid the public in general, and genrally reacts to most people in a verbally, aggressive manner because I feel that he thinks most people will automatically criticise anything he has to say. However, Norman will not discuss these feelings with anyone other than myself at present.	*68*
Case Conference at Oaklands, see minutes on file. Agreed that I should contact G.P. Dr. Moss and Psychiatrist Dr. Cook re Norman's mental state.	14.2.84

Norman Mills listened to me. The staff around me couldn't see me. They were concerned with discipline and order. I didn't want to claim benefits because I was proud of my work ethic. The home insisted I claimed benefits so that I could pay for my keep. But I couldn't sign on for benefits because I couldn't get out of the home.

NOTES TO PATIENT ABOUT USING THIS FORM

You can use this form either:

1. For Statutory Sick Pay (SSP) purposes – fill in Part A overleaf. Also fill in Part B if the doctor has given you a date to resume work. Give or send the completed form to your employer.

2. For Social Security purposes –
To continue a claim for State benefit fill in Parts A and C of the form overleaf. Also fill in Part B if the doctor has given you a date to resume work. **Sign and date the form** and give or send it to your local social security office QUICKLY to avoid losing benefit.

NOTE: To start your claim for State benefit you must use form SCI(Rev) if you are self-employed, unemployed or non-employed OR form SSPI(E) or SSPI(T) if you are an employee. For further details get leaflet NI16 (from DHSS local offices).

Doctor's Statement

In confidence to
Mr/Mrs/Miss/Ms _____ *Lemmn Sissay.* _____

I examined you today/yesterday and advised you that

(a) You need not refrain from work

(b) you should refrain from work

for* *One week.*

OR until ....

Diagnosis of your disorder causing absence from work *Depressive State.*

Doctor's remarks

Doctor's signature *Elliott*

Date of signing *17. 2. 84*

WIGAN Family Practitioner Committee
Dr L. G. N. MOSS
230b Newton R... 133646
Tel. 73962 ...MARY'S,
  ...A3 ...

Form Med 3
3/83

NOTE TO DOCTOR *†See inside front cover for notes on completion.*

20th February, 1984

The Manager,
Sickness Benefits Section,
2 Windemere Rd.,
Leigh.

Dear Sir,

RE: LEMN (NORMAN) SISSAY D.O.B. 21.5.1967
ACCOMMODATED AT 'OAKLANDS' CHILDRENS HOME,
196 NEWTON ROAD, LOWTON

Please find enclosed sickness note in respect of the above named, who moved to
'Oaklands' from our Children's Home at 26 Gregory Ave., Atherton on the 2nd
February, 1984.

Lemn (who is also known as Norman) has been unemployed since January, 1984,
when he ceased employment at Gardeners Clothing Company, Atherton. As far as I
am aware Lemn may not have since signed on for employment. However, it does appear
that this has probably been due to his psychiatric problems which have only now
been recognised by my Department and confirmed by Dr. Moss at Lowton.

For your information, Lemn has been in the care of this Authority almost from birth.
However, since finishing work in January, he has only been receiving pocket money
from my Department, on a weekly basis.

I would be grateful for your attention in this matter.

Yours sincerely,

Mr Sumner, the area officer, declared that a condition has
'only now been recognised by the department and confirmed
by Dr Moss'. He transferred the information from Gregory
Avenue to Oaklands. The reason I wanted the doctor was
so that my condition would be on record. And, at last, I can
see that my plan worked. I asked to see a psychiatrist following
on from the doctor's diagnosis. Nothing felt safe around me.
I needed help. Most of all I needed witnesses. I knew I was
having a breakdown. After sixteen days in Oaklands, Mr
Sumner reported:

RE: NORMAN GREENWOOD D.O.B. (21.5.1967)
OAKLANDS CHILDRENS HOME

An initial Case Conference was held at Oaklands on the 14th February, 1984. Present were Mr. Sumner, Mr. Mills, Mr. Dobbin, Mr. Harding and Care Staff, Norman.

Norman moved to Oaklands from Gregory Avenue on the 2nd February, 1984. His behaviour at Gregory Avenue, had become intolerable and it was felt that Oaklands may be a more appropriate placement for him. Since arrival at Oaklands Norman's behaviour appears to have changed very little - he tends not to fully co-operate, can be stubborn and deliberately provocative in his replies. He seems to feel that staff are against him and at the same time staff are perhaps expecting difficulties and the tension mounts. Norman complains that he has a problem which is known to Mr. Mills and which requires the help of a psychiatrist. He is not prepared to divulge the nature of the problem to anyone else but claims that the problem is making him anti-social e.g. he smashed his guitar, has no friends and refuses to sign on the 'dole' to obtain money to support himself. Reasoning on this issue fails. It was stated at the last conference that if he did not improve then consideration should be given to moving him to Woodend. Although not the majority view, it is felt that this would be premature at this stage and that the expressed psychological difficulties should be investigated.

From the point of view of finance we may have to support him until he obtains a medical certificate or decides to accept 'dole' or finds employment.

CONCLUSIONS

1. Norman to remain at Oaklands for the immediate future.

2. Dr. Moss G.P., to be consulted with regard to Norman's mental health.

3. The possibility of a referral to Dr. Cook, Cons. Psychaitrist to be investigated.

K. B. SUMNER
Area Officer

I'd been in children's homes for four years. I still had no family. I knew that the staff who were supposed to be looking after me were not looking after me at all. On a midnight walk someone shouted at me, 'What you think you're doing round here? Fucking wog. Weirdo.' A few days passed and I saw their pretty garage door and I kicked it. The police came.

Unconnected to this, I had asked to see a psychiatrist. In her first letter to Norman Mills the psychiatrist calls me 'Norman Greenwood (also known as Lemn Sissay)'. In this second letter in March she refers to me as 'Lemn Sissay (known as Norman Greenwood)'.

CHILD AND FAMILY PSYCHIATRY CENTRE

35.

Wigan Health Authority

Wigan Social Services Department

GARSWOOD HOUSE,
ATHERTON ROAD,
HINDLEY,
WIGAN WN2 3EY

Our Ref: PAC/RB.

Your Ref:

Tel: Wigan 59216

8th March 1984.

Mr. Norman Mills,
Metropolitan Borough of Wigan,
Social Services Dept.,
82, High Street,
Golborne,
Nr. Warrington.

Dear Mr. Mills,

Re: Lemn Sissay (also known as Norman Greenwood), d.o.b. 21.5.67.
Oaklands Children's Home.

Thank you for referring Lemn; as you know I was able to see him at Garswood House on 6.3.84, and it was most useful to have your report about his background.

I will not repeat his history, which is well known to you, but over the past two or three months there has been increasing concern about Lemn and also he has been very worried about himself - indeed he told me he had asked to see a psychiatrist as he feared for his sanity. He is an intelligent, articulate boy, who was able to give a good account of himself and his past experiences as well as describing how he thought and felt at the moment. He told me he felt there were two main problems at present, one is an exceptional awareness and self-consciousness to do with his body and the effect he has on other people, and the other is a search for a new and more valid persona, as he feels in the past he has been moulded by other people's expectations of him. One of the difficulties is having rejected the personalities he has assumed in the past he has nothing with which to replace them. Not surprisingly, he has become very interested in the Rastafarian religion and culture but still is not confident enough yet to meet other ethiopians, etc.

I got the impression that Lemn is a person with high ideals of honesty, trust, etc., who feels, with some reason, that many adults in his life have been less than honest with him. He is certainly unhappy and describes the effects of de-personalisation. However, he is also intelligent, has insight, and a sharp sense of humour and these latter make one optimistic about his ability to cope in the future.

Lemn accepted that before he is able to make plans for his future he will have to feel better in himself. I felt it important to reassure him that although he is depressed and unsettled at the present time he is certainly not "mad" nor does he suffer from any formal psychiatric disorder. I offered to see him individually, and this he has accepted.

Yours sincerely,

P.A. Cook.
Consultant Child Psychiatrist.

cc. Dr. Moss.

137

On 20 March 1984 I stood before Leigh Juvenile Court for
kicking the garage door. Norman Mills wrote a three-page
testimony to them, outlining my story with my birth mother
and the Greenwoods:

METROPOLITAN BOROUGH OF WIGAN
SOCIAL SERVICES DEPARTMENT

Social Enquiry Report prepared for the Leigh Juvenile
Court, sitting on Tuesday, 20th March, 1984.

Subject. LEMN SISSAY.   Age 16 years.
        (known as Norman Greenwood)
                                  D.O.B. 21st May, 1967

Home address. Oaklands Children's Home.
             196, NewtonRoad,
             Lowton St. Marys'.

OFFENCE.   CRIMINAL DAMAGE.

Decision of Court.   CONDITIONAL DISCHARGE
                      FOR 1 YEAR.

Details of Family.

		Age.	Address.	Occupation.
Mother	Yemarshet Sissay.	38	Last known address. C/O Ethiopian Union Mission. Addis Ababa. Ethopia.	Not known.
Father.	Nothing known.			
Subject.	Lemn Sissay.	16	Oaklands Children's Home.	Unemployed.
Former Foster Parents.				
	Mr. & Mrs. Greenwood.		2, Osborne Road, Ashton-in-Makerfield.	

(Mr. & Mrs. Greenwood have 3 children of their own.)

Lemn is currently accommodated in Oaklands Children's Home, which is a large
children's home, in Lowton, run by the Wigan Metropolitan Borough Council,
Social Services Department. Lemn has been accommodated there since the 2nd February,
1984, having previously lived in a small Children's home in Atherton for the past
3 years. Although he has his own bedroom, Lemn shares the homes facilities with
all the children in 'Oaklands'.

Lemn has been in the care of Social Services Department since the 30th June, 1967.,
and this authority have had parental rights in respect of this young man since
January, 1971. He has been known as Norman since first coming into care, but has
in the recent past reverted to the Ethiopian Christian name, Lemn, given to him by
his mother.

Lemn is the illegitimate son of an Ethiopian mother, Yemarshet Sissay, and was
born in the Wigan area, during the time when his mother was studying at a Bible
College in England. Miss Sissay was 21 years of age at the time of Lemn's birth,
and requested his reception into care when he was a few weeks old because she
claimed she was unable to care for him. She later returned to Ethipia after her
studies were completed, being aware at that time that Lemn had been placed with
foster parents, a Mr. & Mrs. Greenwood. Miss Sissay has never returned to this
country, although was in contact with Social Services until July, 1968.   276

Contd....

Mr. & Mrs. Greenwood had no family of their own when Lemn was first placed with them at the age of 7 months. They have since had 3 children of their own, the eldest child, Christopher being born when Lemn was about 1 year old. Lemn remained with the Greenwood family until January, 1980, when he moved to Woodfields Children's home, at the age of 12½ years. He has therefore never known any other family life, and to all intents and purpose still sees himself as a member of the Greenwood family, (albeit a rather distant member these days), despite the breakdown of this fostering placement.

Relationships between Lemn and his foster parents had been strained for a long time although basically it was felt that Lemn derived a fair degree of security in the foster home. However, Lemn's reaction to, and non-acceptance of Mr. & Mrs. Greenwood's rather rigid Christian beliefs, appeared eventually to directly lead to the breakdown of this situation. As the boy moved into adolescence, he had begun to question his lack of freedom, relative to his peer group, which had not been well received by the foster parents. Mr. & Mrs. Greenwood showed a great deal of inflexibility and lack of tolerance, in being unable to accept Lemn's rebellion against their Christian beliefs.

Finally, the Greenwoods demanded that Lemn be removed, although they largely rationalised any feelings of guilt that they may have experienced, by pointing out that Lemn himself wanted to leave.

Lemn remained at Woodfields Children's Home, Leigh for a year, before being moved to a small Family Group Home in Gregory Ave, Atherton in January, 1981. The Greenwood family rarely if ever made any attempt to contact him during this time, and contact was therefore maintained almost solely by this Department. The family agreed to Lemn visiting occasionally for the day, although he was made very aware that he would only be allowed to return if he was to conform completely to their demands of him. Lemn therefore declined to visit the Greenwood family after a time, and appeared to feel a strong feeling of rejection by the 'family' coupled with feelings of guilt. He certainly appeared to pass through a period of general depression, when the realisation of his situation finally became all to apparent to him.

Work with Lemn at the time therefore revolved around helping him come to terms with the reality of the situation, which included accepting the fact that his 'family' were largely to blame for his rejection. Lemn has since formed a very accurate picture of the Greenwood's personal shortcomings, and has displayed considerable insight into their attitudes and behaviour towards him. Despite everything However, Lemn still retains some loyalty to the Greenwood family and visits them very occasionally. The foster family however have not contacted Lemn for some years to my knowledge.

The past 12 months have been particularly difficult for Lemn, as various situations appeared to have continued to contribute to his general feeling of isolation. Lemn left school in May, 1983 - having obtained 6 C.S.E. passes. He was an extremely popular young man at school, but unfortunately he did not attain the level of academic performance of which he was capable. 277

Contd....

152

Lemn had largely discounted the value of academic achievements, because for some years before leaving school he had been working on Saturdays for a local businessman who had undoubtedly convinced him that he would help him to start up his own business. This gentleman had built up Lemns expectations quite considerably, but unfortunately he then appeared to withdraw many of his promises to this young man, and Lemn parted company with the gentleman and his family, with whom he had previously been very close. Shortly afterwards Lemn went into the man's warehouse and deliberately damaged some of his stock – causing damage to the value of £9.80. This was the first occasion on which Lemn had been charged with an offence, and in my opinion, was largely occasioned by his strong feelings of rejection by the businessman involved. Lemn received a caution for this offence.

During the past year, Lemn had also seen his relationship deteriorate with the officer in charge of the small children's Home, in Atherton, where he lived, and he had lost contact with many of his former friends who were also in Care. Towards the end of 1983, Lemn obtained employment in a local factory through his own efforts, and he worked there for about 2 months. Unfortunately however, this young man then gave up his job in January, 1984 because he no longer felt capable of performing it. It does appear that Lemn has gradually suffered from depression and anxiety over the past few months, and that his former confidence and self-image have been considerably damaged. As a result, he is currently receiving medical help for this condition.

Attitude Towards Offence.

Lemn has readily admitted to the offence for which he appears before the Court today, He has however explained that he committed the offence in retaliation for being described previously as a 'wog' by the owner of the garage door in question.

Conclusion.

Lemn Sissay is an intelligent, sensitive young man, who as your Worships will appreciate, has suffered from a great deal of rejection during his short life-time. His rejection by his foster family at the age of 12 years, was not of his making, but was largely attributable to their own shortcomings. Subsequently, and particularly in the past 12 months, he has experienced further breakdowns in relationships, which he sees also as rejections, and which have badly affected his self confidence. He is particularly sensitive to any sort of 'implied' criticism at present, but this is all part and parcel of the depressed condition he has experienced for the past few months apparently. He is a very isolated young man, who has no strong family ties on which to fall back on.

This offence occurred only recently, when Lemn was very low in spirits, and at a time when he was also facing the anxiety of being moved to another children's home. He has obviously coped in the past with racial prejudice without resorting to this sort of behaviour, and I feel that he is capable of avoiding a repetition of this behaviour. I would therefore respectfully request your Worships to consider imposing a Conditional Discharge for this offence.

Mr. N. Mills.
Senior Social Worker.

153

This is a spirited defence of a sixteen-year-old boy having a breakdown. I received a one-year conditional discharge. Within days The Authority arrived and called a 'staff meeting with appropriate social workers regarding control'. This really was *1984*.

STAFF MEETING WITH APPROPRIATE SOCIAL WORKERS REGARDING CONTROL

Present: Mr. J. Harding, Officer-in-Charge, Oaklands
House Parents, Oaklands
Mr. B. Roberts, Residential Manager
Mr. N. Mills, Senior Social Worker, Golborne
Mrs. J. Jones, Social Worker, Leigh

Mr. Roberts opened the Meeting by stating its purpose was to discuss control problems with older children and if possible get feed back from Social Workers of children's attitudes and feelings towards Oaklands and any suggestions which may help to remedy the control problems at the Home.

Some time was spent discussing Norman Greenwood as his behaviour gave staff most concern. Oaklands staff mentioned that Norman tended to lead some of the young children astray, was generally disruptive and had been involved recently in various escapades such as being up late at night after staff had gone to bed and climbing scaffolding outside of the building. Behavioural problems with Norman have been a long standing problem, both at Oaklands and at Gregory Avenue, where he was previously placed. Recently, however, some light has been shed on the behavioural problems and it appears that Norman is suffering from some form of depression and has, generally speaking, psychiatric problems. Mr. Mills said that despite Norman's poor behaviour he was always a truthful boy and if he had done anything wrong, he would always admit it.

Staff complained that Norman tended to irritate them by nudging them and bumping into them and generally being disruptive. Mr. Mills replied that Norman tended to want physical contact and perhaps this could, he realised, in some cases, cause staff embarrassment

A lengthy discussion was then pursued about Norman and his history, but the Meeting could not find an answer to Norman's behavioural problems and the emphasis appeared to be more on how to react after he had been caught mis-behaving.

154

I was in a tailspin. On the one hand I had The Authority hounding me with a threat of Wood End; on the other I had the police. May 21 would be my seventeenth birthday, which left me twelve months until the care system was going to throw me out. I hated Oaklands. I hated John Harding.

Norman seen on all these occasions - I have continued to take him to see Dr Moss and Dr Cook, as he is still unwilling /unable to make these journeys on his own.
Norman has assurred me however that he is feeling better within himself mentally. He is beginning to regain his enjoyment of life - whereas until fairly recently he has often been slightly depressed and unhappy. However, he has made the occasional trip- into Leigh and Ashton and he has now rejoined the 'Who Cares' group in Leigh, although this time on his own terms. Instead of allowing Leslie Jenkinson to dominate the group with her own negative attitudes - Norman has apparently tried to steer the group in what I feel would be a more positive direction.

| 10.4.84 |
| 19.4.84 |
| 26.4.84 |
| 30.4.84 |
| 8.5.84 |
| 10.5.84 |
| 17.5.84 |
| 21.5.84 |
| 22.5.84 |
| ENTERE |

Norman has also made contact with the 'Naypic' Group and hopes that they may publish some of his poems. He appears to derive benefit from his visits to see Dr Cook and he feels that she does understand his problems of identity/culture crisis. Dr Cook is attempting to link Norman up with a group of coloured adolescents in the Manchester area - which he himself desires (although is very nervous of).

Norman has written to the Seventh Day Adventist Church in Ethiopia and was overjoyed to receive a reply which stated that his natural mother is now living in Ghana, West Africa. The Mission in Ethiopia have promised to try to contact Normans mother. I have shared more of her letters with Norman - particularly relating to the time (1968) when she tried to regain his care but was refused (virtually) by Wigan CB, Childrens Dept.

Normans behaviour and attitudes towards the Oaklands staff unfortunately do not improve.   with

                                        I beleive that, he has also damaged a bed by jumping on to it - generally messes about at night. He has again gone off for most of the night on one occasion, this following a row with the Greenwood family. Norman incidentally has acquired a steady (white) girl friend who is 17 and working. She comes from Ashton and is named Diane.

Normans clothing continues to be a problem and Mr Lee and Mr Wilson have assured me that the Homes Clothing account cannot provide items for Norman. I have therefore applied to Mr Hulme (DO Fieldwork) for clothing on a C.P. 28 but to date do not have an answer.

                    N. Mills, Senior Social Worker

These notes precede and follow on from my seventeenth birthday. No one made the connection. I returned to the Greenwoods to ask for photographs. My foster mother sat me in the posh room, like a visitor, and opened the photo albums. She shielded the photographs from my sightline as a child shields his food at the school dinner table to protect his chips from being pinched. I felt belittled. I had no proof of my childhood. I needed photographic evidence that I once belonged somewhere. There were no photographs taken in the children's home either. Catherine carefully extracted four photographs. She closed the album and asked me to leave. But I had more questions about my birth mother. My foster mother flew into a rage and slammed the album on the floor. She phoned my social worker and demanded he take me away. She threw me out of the house and I waited for him on the front step.

I hadn't 'acquired a steady (white) girlfriend'. Diane was my first girlfriend. We met in the first year of comprehensive school when I was twelve and lived with my foster parents. She had no idea where I'd disappeared to when they took me away. She called my foster mum but she wouldn't tell Diane. Diane searched for me for years and found me. We are close friends to this day. In fact, our friendship is the longest close relationship I've ever known.

I ran away from Oaklands at night. I walked the East Lancs Road to Moss Side in Manchester – nearly fourteen miles away. I sat inside the doorway of a record shop a little further up from the Reno nightclub. It was 2 a.m. and I watched

156

people talking walking laughing. Beautiful dark faces. The bass was making the world vibrate into the summer air.

But I looked quite threatening, bedraggled, wild-eyed and fearful. There was some suspicion about the guy in the doorway. It was me. A pirate taxi-driver took a long look as he slid along the kerb. Time to go. I arrived back at Oaklands at daybreak to the police.

SW
21.6.84

Norman returned to Oaklands today and later brought back tent and sleeping bag. Apparently after returning he had been flicking lighted matches at the curtains which had caused them to be slightly burnt. A Case Conference was held this afternoon (report on file) at which the decision was taken to move Norman to Woodend for a period of assessment.

I can't remember flicking matches or burning any curtains. I've never been accused of doing anything like it before or since. There's no mention of my diagnosis or my attendance to the doctor or psychiatrist. This report is from Oaklands on 17 May, four days before my seventeenth birthday.

17-6-84   Norman failed to return. Police informed 11.25pm.
At 4.50 am the A.L.U telephoned to say that Norman was next door, he was sent through and he was asked where he had been, he said 'about'. When the police came to see him he said he had been at Mrs. Greenwood's until 10.30pm.

Norman has been climbing the scaffolding at Oaklands again, as well as staying out overnight. He told me that he had a fierce argument with the Greenwood family late on Sunday night (17.6.84) which had so 'fired' him up., that he had wandered around Ashton and Lowton for the rest of the night. He was in a difficult mood today, and insisted to Mr. Harding and I for some time that he had not received his latest Giro. Despite all our attempts to get him to accept that it was obvious that Norman had cashed his Giro (Norman has had £10 notes on him this week), Norman would not admit to having done this, although he obviously saw the whole matter as something of a joke.

SPECIAL CONFERENCE ON NORMAN GREENWOOD

PRESENT: Mr. B. Roberts, Manager Residential Services
              Mr. B. Sumner, Area Officer, Golborne
              Mr. N. Mills
              Mr. J. Harding
              Mrs. Y. Smalley
              Miss M. Runciman
              Miss M. Cafferty
              Miss C. Allmond

The consensus of opinion from Oaklands staff was that Norman would not conform to any discipline whatsoever. He was influencing the younger children by showing a bad example which in turn could lead to mass disruption at Oaklands.

A decision was to be made as to the alternative accommodation available as it was felt that Norman could no longer remain at Oaklands. Also, when the decision was made how best to inform him of it.

Discussion took place about Normans reasons for non-conforming. It was felt that Norman needed protection against himself and others from him for whatever reason he was rebelling.

    1) Because he had no control over his actions

or 2) Because they are deliberate acts against authority.

Mr. Mills then informed the group of his reasons for placing Norman at Oaklands. Although he felt it was not the ideal situation, he wanted somewhere not too far away from Gregory Avenue so that Norman could maintain links with his friends/associates.

Mention was made that Dr. Cook (who was not present) had been trying to link Norman up with a group of coloured people in Manchester, the idea being that he could be accommodated in a Hostel with people who were more in tune with the culture that Norman was pursuing. However, this idea was dismissed because senior management would not agree to fund it. A suggestion was made that Dr. Cook could approach senior management again and make a strong recommendation towards Norman being accommodated in a hostel in Manchester and the detrimental effect if steps were not taken.

In conclusion, the conference felt that because Norman's behaviour was having a gross adverse effect on the other children in the Home, and that his actions were deemed to be often of a dangerous nature, for example, flicking lighted matches about. There was no alternative but to remove Norman from Oaklands. The conference decided that a period of assessment in a more disciplined environment such as Wood End would be necessary to help resolve Norman's problems.

Mr. Roberts, therefore, made arrangements for Norman to be transferred to Wood End this evening.

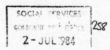

WOOD END

CHAPTER 28

Connect cold ice with fire
And the ice melts to find
Broken telephone wires
Tangled in Mangled Minds.

We ran like the water
Cupped in hands
And splashed like the water
That splits lands

The date of the decision by The Authority to imprison me in Wood End was 21 June 1984. There were no charges. No sentence. I was taken immediately. Norman Mills drove me through Lowton, Leigh and Atherton, onto Everest Road and through the gates of Wood End Assessment Centre.

We were both silent. He didn't want me in there. He knew it was a foregone conclusion even before I went to Oaklands from Gregory Avenue. I had been in 'care' of Wigan Social Services for seventeen years. The idea that they wanted to assess me *now* was a joke. This wasn't assessment. This was imprisonment.

The staff at Wood End told Norman Mills he couldn't come in. He wanted to check where I would be sleeping and eating for his report but the rules were different at Wood End. There was a smirk on the officer's face. 'Welcome to Wood End, young man. We do things differently here.'

I was marched to a utility room. A seriously overweight man with a thick bunch of keys slapped down some regulation clothes – 'different clothes for a different place'. A three-button T-shirt, dark blue trousers and pumps, all in the muted colours of rubbish that's gone through a mangle. He told me to bathe and change. I was marched to the sports hall and sat at a table. The food came in one tray with bowls moulded into it. I ate with a plastic fork and spoon. Wood End was deathly silent. There were no pictures on the walls. After eating they led me through grey fire doors, more security, to the medical room for a health check with Mrs M., under her cloying leer. I was being reprogrammed.

'You have one hour a day of recreation,' the man said. He opened the door into a plain room with chairs lined against the walls where boys were sitting. They barely looked up. Unlock. Lock. Unlock. Lock. I was taken deeper inside. A siren went off. A howling raced through the corridors. 'Testing the alarm,' said the man.

There were two sorts of child-inmates: young people on remand (awaiting court appearances) and young people in care. It was a technical difference because we were all treated like charged criminals. I was under surveillance twenty-four hours a day. I was marched along the corridors in size order with the others, largest at the front, smallest at the back. In silence. We were to speak when spoken to. The assessment centre's job was to keep us in order all times – meal times, recreation, gardening and education. Anyone who stepped out of line was beaten. There was no 'outside' now. This was a lock-up.

The officers were mainly men. White men. Men who wanted to be somewhere else. Men who didn't hide their displeasure in us. Men who viewed us as weaklings. Men who got a rush out of fighting. Ex-police officers, ex-probation officers, ex-army officers. Men with moustaches and pot-bellies. Weight-lifting men with chipmunk cheeks and over-stacked chests. White men with white fists. Men who stood like bouncers outside clubs. White men with white smirks and yellow teeth. Men in the middle of divorces, men with drinking problems, men with sexual problems, men trying to forget that they were not who they wanted to be when they were boys like us; men with crotch rot and athlete's foot. Men with anger issues. Broken men. Hurt men. Dangerous, white men. Men who hated their fathers.

This really was George Orwell's *1984*. I was right. I was right about the entire dysfunctional system, which pretended it could care for me while knowing in its heart that it couldn't. This horrific place was where the system stopped pretending.

Reprogramming meant I had to have a psychological test to determine whether I would be put into labour or education. It was my human right not to be imprisoned and therefore nothing in the assessment centre had any validity in my eyes, including the staff.

But I had to be careful to avoid a beating. How to comply and yet not comply? The test asked questions such as, *Are you a tree in a forest or a tree on a hill?* I replied, *I am a poet tree.* The hierarchy were displeased.

Remember that I knew I should not have been in Wood End. I knew The Authority did not have the intelligence to deal with me. And most of all, I knew that challenging them, in Wood End, on any of these issues would incur their wrath.

Are you a tree in a forest or a tree on a hill? The questions offended me so I answered them *my* way. Because of this, Wood End brought in a school psychologist to assess me.

Schools Psychological Service,
Orrell Lodge,
Orrell Mount,
Orrell,
Wigan

12th July 1984

Dear Mr. Mackey,

Lemn Sissay (D.O.B. 21.5.67)

Thank you for asking me to see this young man whose behaviour at Oaklands and general hostility have led to a placement at Wood End.

I have chosen to write to you rather than to do a conventional report as I have no psychological test results to comment upon or interpret and, in view of my limited acquaintance with Lemn, would feel unable to offer more than an impression of his personality and problems.

As you know Lemn answered some of the questionnaires and completed most of the tests in a non-serious way. He also rejected the idea of completing an individual intelligence test for me. The reason he gave for this rejection of the tests was that such tests could not give a true picture of him as an individual and might be used to make decisions for him which he preferred to make for himself. I think that he was casting doubt on the validity of the tests and the psychometric process and although not a point of view that I personally subscribe to, it is certainly not untenable nor is it unreasonable for an intelligent person to adopt. However the motivation for rejecting assessment is not intellectual but part of a growing (?) rejection of the 'care' concept, i.e. of other people making decisions for him.

Lemn is very much into self-identification. He is interested in his Ethiopian roots (familial and historical) and in some of the concepts and attitudes of Rastafarianism which offer black consciousness and black pride in a cultural context.

When he was asked to write about himself he commented that "life ... seems like a documentary on television" - which appears to me to be an expression of alienation. He decided to write a poem to, as he says, "capture a piece of emotion". The poem reads as follows:-

> "They told me
> This was me, my family, my home
> But i still ended up, alone
> Once again i packed my smaller suitcase
> Another loss of trust on a wild goose chase
> Like a knot in a shoe lace,
> They thought they did it best
> But the more they pulled the harder the case
> And who ended up with less
>
> And now through the jungle of paper theory and pen
> I just only find out my name is Lemn
> An i bin cheated beated pushed and hit
> Now mi name a Lemn and de fire bin lit
> Now after i learnt dem say i mus' learn
> Throw water on the fire but the fire still burn".

The spirit of Bob Marley lives on! I applaud Lemn's courage but am not convinced that the choices he makes will be very sensible. He is better off making his own mistakes, given some degree of support, than having decisions made on his behalf.

Yours sincerely,

J. Yates
Principal Educational Psychologist

The Authority was not happy with the letter from the educational psychologist and a few days later they made their own report. It was most important for them to record that I was nothing special.

Metropolitan Borough of Wigan

Social Services Department

ASSESSMENT CENTRE

J.G. Poyner D.M.A., F.C.I.S., M.B.I.M.
Director of Social Services

Superintendent:
Mr. N. Mackey

Matron:
Mrs. J. Benson
Tel. No. Atherton 884621

"Wood End",
Everest Road,
Atherton,
Manchester.
M29 9NT

.19th July........................19 84.

Lemn SISSAY (D.O.B. 21.5.67)

Schoolroom test results

Chronological Age	17 years 1 month
Arithmetic Age (Vernon – Senior)	15 years 6 months
Reading Age (Schonell Word Recognition)	15 years +
Reading Experience (Daniels & Diack)	13 years 1 month
Comprehension Age (Schonell B)	8 years 11 months
Composition Age	15 year old level
General Knowledge	12/40
I.Q. (N.F.E.R.iii)	90

Initial Impressions and Reaction to Testing

Sissay treated the testing procedure with complete and utter contempt. Although the initial numeracy and literacy tests were answered fairly sensibly, the later tests, particularly the psychological ones, evoked a series of responses ranging from the glib to the absurd. The reliability of his overall scores is thus questionable, but it is probably not unfair to conclude that he is a youth of around average intelligence, both numerate and literate.

General Comments

It has been evident since his admission to Wood End that Sissay has found the experience of the structured environment somewhat unwelcome. His attitude towards both the routine and the tasks he has been required to fulfil has ranged between the easy-going 'laid-back' approach to outright contempt.

At best he is a relaxed, friendly youth, able to converse intelligently and respond in a good-humoured manner. He holds strong views on Rastafarianism, but because he is inclined to be intolerant of others' views, arguments with staff have resulted.

Generally though, he has exercised restraint and has conformed to the routine requirements of the establishment. On occasions, however, when he has been given a task not to his liking, or when not in the mood, his underlying contempt has become more overt. This has been most noticeable on the sports field where he has either spurned efforts to get him to compete or has sabotaged the efforts of his team mates with displays of sportsmanship totally unrelated to his ability.

His relationships with other boys in Wood End have been mostly friendly.
Because of his size, colour and sporting prowess, he has been a natural focus
of attention and is regarded with a certain degree of awe particularly by the
younger element.

Considering Sissay's age it is unlikely that education will play any further
part in his future. It would seem that he needs a degree of guidance
towards some form of meaningful occupation.

G. Honeybone
Teacher

'Sportsmanship totally unrelated to his ability.' This means that I happily gave the football to a lesser player (sportsmanship) rather than took the opportunity to run with it. I saw how the staff played football with us and how aggressive they were. It seemed to me they were working out their own mental problems and we were just a backdrop. It was belittling to see them joyously slicing the legs of young boys as if they were playing amongst men. It was sick. I trained myself in indifference. Many of the boys felt free in sport but I saw how much the staff enjoyed hurting them. Let them play, I thought. These people may have had us physically locked up. But they couldn't have my mind.

The dormitories were locked at night. It is the only time we were without constant supervision. Because of the red nightlight in our rooms we couldn't see out of the meshed glass slit in the dormitory door, but the night watchman could see in.

What must we have looked like to him when we were fast asleep? Young boys from eleven to eighteen, our heads resting on pillows, our hands gripping the sheets to our necks, mouths slightly open with the night-light splashing the shadows from our eyelashes across our faces.

There were women who worked at Wood End under the eyes of the men. But they were syphoned of their instincts. I have had nightmares up until my forties that I was still imprisoned in Wood End. Dickens hinted of the same condition when his father had been placed in debtors' jail and he found himself in a similar destitute institution – the workhouse. Dickens wrote:

The deep remembrance of the sense I had of being utterly neglected and hopeless; of the shame I felt in my position; of the misery it was to my young heart to believe that, day to day, what I had learned, and thought, and delighted in, and raised my fancy and my emulation up by, was passing away from me, never to be brought back any more; cannot be written. My whole nature was so penetrated with the grief and humiliation of such considerations, that even now, famous and caressed and happy, I often forget in my dreams that I have a dear wife and children; even that I am a man; and wander desolately back to that time of my life . . .

Wood End was a nightmare of unimaginable proportions, and it caused nightmares. It is easy to wonder if this happened at all. Years later, in 2013, I wrote a blog about Wood End. I didn't expect what followed. Other people reached out. This gives you a better picture than I could. Kevin on 15 November 2014 at 3.57 p.m. said:

I was dumped there by the council while my mother was in hospital when I was 12. I had never been in trouble or had any contact with the police, but by the time I left that place I was a broken child. I have never got over it. It has affected everything I have done in my life. Today I am contacting Wigan council and Manchester police to have my say as well. I have managed to raise a family, send my two kids to university, and have had my own business for the last 20 years but I lived with a life of demons, in the past using drugs, I have bouts of depression, an ongoing struggle against alcohol, low self-esteem, self-destructive anger problems. I have been one of the lucky ones. Those people who abused us were the weak and the useless, not us.

Ricky Mayes on 8 February 2015 at 12.49 p.m. said:

My life has never been the same in and out of mental hospitals all my life brain injury due to having my head smashed against the black board in maths class no dr was called I was knocked unconscious for over 24 hours I have got a on going investigation going on with Manchester police I was just a innocent child like your self at the time if you want to contact me please do. wish I knew the name of the maths teacher in 1977 I want him and all the other staff brought to justice for the abuse mental physical and sexual that I and many other boys suffered under Wood Ends sick regime lets stand together and have a voice.

Nick on 10 May 2014 at 12.26 p.m. said:

I was at Wood End between 1979 and 1981. One staff member was a bully. I got my first kicking on my second day there, one of many. I was forced to strip and had my genitals and rectum fondled and examined (that's what he called it). Once refused to eat my porridge because I didn't like the pink packets of low calorie sugar they used, I wanted some proper sugar. So once the hall was cleared I was held behind and had my face pushed into the porridge and held there until I agreed to eat it. My face was marked for about 2 weeks.

Got into an almighty row with the member of staff, a few hours after my case conference was heard, as I was told I could speak to my mum before she left, they never let me see her. He pushed me against the corridor wall outside his office and held me there by my testicles squeezing them harder and harder, it seemed to last a life time. It made me vomit all over his jacket, to which I was given a good stomach punch which left me on the floor crying and in agony. The following day he told me I would never see my home again or my parents should I tell anyone what had happened, he said he could keep me in care forever, I believed him, I was 14 and none the wiser. Throughout my stays at Wood End I was made to strip, had my genitals fondled and was punched or beaten at least once a week. I went from Wood End to St Thomas More at Birkale Southport.

Things there were not as regimental as Wood End but the abuse was worse, regular body checks by one member of staff, included having you genitals played with and a finger or two inserted into your rectum.

Colleen Candland on 10 February 2015 at 6.44 a.m. said:

My husband was in care from the age of 10. Wood End was a care home he was placed in on two occasions. He has the physical scars which were the result of the malicious and very violent beatings. He also ran away from Wood End, jumping directly through the glass window of the dorm and leaving a chunk of his skin on the broken window pane. He was caught 9 hours later in an old mill. He was taken by the police to the hospital for stitches to his damaged hand then he was returned to Wood End. Only terror could make a child jump through a glass pane to escape the brutality. He was in care all of his childhood and did become one of the many who did end up in prison. The emotional pain is still buried deep within and will never be erased. He has first-hand experience of the cruelty administered by the staff in the homes and has never forgotten their faces or names. On a positive note he has made a life for himself and has found happiness. He is now works as a falconer and the care and love he bestows on his birds and dogs is beautiful to see and experience, particularly when you know how much pain he carries within his soul. He will not talk to the police or any of the authorities as he does not seek to open his wounds but he does share the horror of his past with me and agreed to me sharing this with you as he has read your blogs, poems and writings and can relate to all of them.

Wood End was a violent and toxic place with a barely hidden general belief that these boys needed to be taught a lesson. The short sharp shock treatment was an alternative term for abuse. In the sports hall they forced us to play 'murder ball'. It was institutionalised violence for voyeurs. I made myself a witness. When a fight broke out between the boys I watched the men, the staff, ejaculate. The men let the fight continue until they'd done. Then they'd say, 'Come on, you two, break it up.' Then they'd watch them in the showers.

One of the boys had been hauled off for going over the top, not even allowed to get showered. I asked where he was off to. The boy next to me muttered, 'Where d'you think? He's getting worked over.'

'Where?'

'In the gym, that's where they like doing it. After that he'll be in the quiet room.' The 'quiet room' was a padded cell.

What were you doing when you were seventeen?

CHAPTER 29

Be the river to the sea
Be a lake to light
Be warm be dawn
Be my satellite

I try to keep sane. I try not to get my head smashed in by The Men. Many years later Norman Mills, my social worker, tells me in a BBC TV documentary, 'You shouldn't have been in there, Lemn.' He also tells me that his colleague apologised to him because the decision was out of their hands too. All of this was down to the Director of Social Services.

I grew my dreadlocks in Wood End. I twist my Afro hair each night at Wood End. I write every day in recreation hour. I have written poems ever since I came into care. They become my flags in the mountainside. They chart the journey. If you think all of this is too crazy to be true then so did I. In my writing there are no limits, no boundaries to the imagination. There is a freedom. My hair rises into a knotted mass of twisted spikes and then the locks drop into a crown of dreadlocks.

Name.................... NORMAN SISSAY ....   Case No.

REMARKS	Initials
Norman is coping with the regime of Woodend, although is not very happy in this establishment. He is kept generally occupied by the staff in doing various jobs in the grounds, although is not allowed out by himself. Norman at least has a general respect for the staff who he feels are 'straight' with him. He prefers to be treated honestly, although this obviously can be quite painful at times. Norman is still insisting that he wishes to leave Woodend as soon as possible after his Case Conference is held.	SW

I have explained to Norman that I feel he would best be placed in a semi independent living unit e.g. a hostel for adolescents with perhaps a separate flat accommodation. Unfortunately, this would mean Norman having to move away from Wigan, and would also require the financial support of this Authority. Norman is unsure of what he wants, although he is obviously anxious about moving away.

I have discussed Norman's future with Dr. Cook and also with Mr. Roberts, Residential Manager. Dr. Cook does not believe that Norman is sufficiently emotionally secure to live on his own, and believes that this type of move could lead him to become depressed easily. She agrees that a semi independent living situation in a hostel for example would appear to be best suited to Norman's needs. Dr. Cook has also now given me the name of a group of black young people in Manchester, the Abasindi Co-op, St. Marys St., Moss Side (Tel: 061-226-6837) and has asked me to arange a meeting with this group for Norman. Dr. Cook can now not attend the forthcoming Case Conference at Woodend.

Mr. Roberts is aware of the difficulties in obtaining a place in a hostel in the Manchester area for Norman, but feels that this Authority would listen to an approach, if the Case Conference and Dr. Cook were to recommend this.

Phoned Dr. Moss' surgery, and explained that Norman would not be keeping an appointment today, because of his changed circumstances. I also phoned D.H.S.S. explained the change of home for this young man. D.H.S.S. want Norman to visit their Leigh Office to complete forms confirming his current living situation. Have subsequently discussed this with Woodend staff.   17.7.84

              N. MILLS. S.S.W.

Attended Norman's Case Conference, which Norman also came into at the end. (See full conference report on the file). Before the Conference, Norman told me that certain staff at Woodend had suggested the possibility of him having his own bedsit/flat within Woodend, whilst he went out to work (or further education studies). Norman has jumped at this possibility and says that he is still too conscious about moving away from the area. This possibility was therefore discussed fully at the Conference, and will be followed up in the near future, when Mr. Mackie returns.   25.7.84

Escorted Norman to and from Dr. Cooks clinic. He is already beginning to backtrack slightly on his request to stay at Woodend yesterday, but I have explained to him that the situation will need further discussion and he will need to be patient. I have arranged an appointment for him at D.H.S.S. on the 30th July and he feels sufficiently confident in himself now to go on his own.   26.7.84

174

Penny Cook, the psychologist, had found information on the National Association of Young People In Care (NAYPIC) and the Abasindi Co-operative which was a black women's theatre group in Moss Side, Manchester. She passed the information to Norman Mills, who passed it to me.

I wrote a pleading letter to a determined, quietly spoken woman called Margaret Parr. She was based in Manchester and worked with NAYPIC. She set up an affiliated organisation called Black and In Care. My first visitor. She came all the way from Manchester to this godforsaken lock-up to visit me, someone she had never met.

Visitor protocol. The sports hall was lined with tables. The staff stood at the front, the sides and the back of the room. We boys were marched in and placed by our seats. 'Sit.' We sat facing forward and waited. Meanwhile our visitors were searched at Reception then escorted through the corridors to the sports hall entrance.

Margaret Parr looked at me before sitting. She rummaged in her bag and brought out a punnet of grapes. I'd asked for grapes. She was the first outside person who could see the shit I was in. I was an experiment that hadn't worked. I had the evidence. But she believed me straightaway.

'There are many of us,' she said, 'all around the country. Black kids fostered or adopted then thrown back into a care system when we reach twelve or so.' Her skin was lighter than mine. She had been in care too.

'This isn't right,' I said. 'They say I am here because they are waiting to put me in a flat but it's been ages and *this is a prison.*'

Margaret could see what it was. 'Don't let them drug you,' she whispered.

Afterwards we lined up in the sports hall. Many of these boys would have just seen their mums or dads or sisters or brothers. We took off our clothes down to our underwear and prepared for the strip search.

Margaret had brought me a book. It was a biography of Bob Marley, by Timothy White. I had read the biography by Ernest Cashmore but this was much better. I read it in recreation time. This was a deeper Marley, the mixed-race boy from the country conquering the harsh glare of Trenchtown. As I read some more of his internal distress I started to understand him more. And the more I felt I understood him, the less I knew. He is a natural mystic.

Margaret told me about two conferences on the horizon which I wanted to attend. One was for the Black and In Care group and the other was at Ruskin College in Oxford for the National Association of Young People In Care. Offering no reason, The Authority said I had to choose one or the other.

Visited today, andhad a full discussion with Norman and Mr. Mackie. 14.9.84
(Visit has been delayed by my absence from work through illness).
We are all agreed that Mr. Mackie will discuss the following
possibilities with Mr. Poynter (Deputy Director) at their meeting ENTERE
next week.

1. The possibility of Norman moving into his own room within Woodend.
2. The question of whether Norman will be allowed to attend the NAPIC conference at Oxford (28/30 Sept. 84) and another one day 61 conference on 20th October, in London (Black-in Care).
3. The possibility of Norman being allowed to start a gutter cleaning business from Woodend. This involves issues such as insurance, liability of the Authority etc.

Norman was reasonably satisfied with these points, although
still unhappy at his lack of freedom to come and go from
Woodend despite his assessment period having been completed.
I understood and sympathise with the lads situation, and hope
that we as an Authority can ~~realise~~ the usual Woodend restrictions
on Norman where possible.

| | SW |

Phoned Woodend, spoke to Mr. Bailey. He said that the 3 issues
discussed with Mr. Poynter had all been received favourably, and
will now be considered by Senior Management. Meanwhile, Norman is
following up possibilities for starting his own business by getting
estimates for insurance, and printing of leaflets etc.

19.9.84

Have discussed the ongoing situation with Dr. Cook, who is quite
pleased to hear of developments. Norman has obviously been telling
of his frustrations at Woodend, and of the delay at implementing
the Case Conference recommendations.

25.9.84
her

Mr. Sumner (A.O.) has been informed by Senior Management today
that Norman will be allowed to attend one or the other of the two
conferences, but I understood not both of them. The Authority wish
to know which of the two Norman will choose to attend. I visited
Norman today and put the choice to him. He insisted that he
wished to attend both, although I had explained the choice. Norman
queried whether management decision was on grounds of finance, which
I was unsure about, although I did make him aware that the
practical difficulties of the one day Conference were worrying the
Authority. norman wishes to attend Ruskin College this weekend
and I therefore discussed the practical arrangements with Norman and
Mr. Mackie. He intends to go with Margaret Parr from
Manchester, and we therefore discussed ways of contacting her
to confirm all the arrangements. I have no paperwork at all re
this Confernece, although Mr. Mackie has had papers on the other
Conference (which he has retained). He and I have had some
disagreements on the handling of this situation, which is
excacerbated by the fact that all my information is arriving at
2nd or 3rd hand.

However, I said that I would confirm arrangements for Norman and
would obtain and deliver a travel warrant for him by the 27th Sept.

Delivered travel warrant to Woodend. I have contacted Margaret
Parr, who has confirmed travel arrangements for Norman and herself.
From her I obtained the organisers names and telephone numbers.
Therefore I have 'phoned NAYPIC at London and Bradford (HQ).
Although I didn't manage to obtain the main organiser, Mr. Leon
Parker, the NAYPIC H.Q. felt that everything would be in order, and
said they would send literature. NAYPIC were allowing for additional
arrivals anyway.

27.9.84

Literature received from NAYPIC.

1.10.84

Letter received from NAYPIC confirming that Norman played a full
part in the Conference, and commenting on the quality of his
poetry.

9.10.84

73

N. MILLS. S.S.W.

Thank God for pressure groups. Had it not been for NAYPIC and WHO CARES and Black and In Care and the Abasindi Co-op I am not sure I would be here today.

At the NAYPIC conference in Oxford there were young people from children's homes and foster care from all over the country. It was breathtaking to be around so many people who had similar experiences.

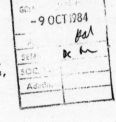

N.A.Y.P.I.C

Head Office: Salem House, 28a Manor Row, Bradford BD1 4QU
Tel. (0274) 728484/733134

SOCIAL SERVICE
GO
– 9 OCT 1984

Please reply to:-

3rd October 1984.

Mr. Mills,
Senior Social Worker,
Wigan Social Services,
82, High Street,
Golborne,
Nr. Warrington.

Dear Mr. Mills,

I hope you received the information about the weekend conference at Ruskin College, Oxford. Lemy found the conference very useful and was involved in the video workshop aswell as the general discussion. His poetry is something to be proud of and I hope he continues with it.

I mentioned to him about the meeting we are holding in Manchester and hope he will be able to attend as he was interested in it. Please see enclosed details.

He is definately wanting to attend the Black and In Care conference on the 20th October 1984 and would be of great value.

If I can be of any further help please don't hesitate to contact me.

Kindest regards,

Charlie Maynard,
Development Officer - North Region.

The Black and In Care conference was a different matter altogether.

I was eventually allowed to attend the Black and In Care conference on 20 October 1984. It was a historical occasion – the first conference for black young people in care. From this conference came the Black and In Care video, which was watched by many social services departments around the country. Exhilarated, I returned to Wood End where I was strip-searched.

CHAPTER 30

In the way light talks to a river
In the way a river holds night beneath
In the way spring calms winter
In this way we should speak

I had a plan all along. The system at Wood End run by The Men was based on privileges. I gained 'privileges' for 'good behaviour'. Privileges meant I could work unsupervised digging the gardens of the staff homes which lined the driveway. So I ran away to the housing office of Atherton Town Hall. I straightened up and approached reception.

'Hi. Can I see the housing officer? It's urgent.' I said this with my best smile.

'What's your name?'

'Peter . . .' I saw a leaflet on the board for the Royal Bank of Scotland. 'Peter Banks.' I hated that lie.

Eventually I was ushered from the waiting room.

'My name is Lemn Sissay. It's not Peter Banks. And I need to tell you I am in Wood End, you know Wood End? And they are saying that they are waiting to find me accommodation. But I shouldn't be there. And I have no family. And it's a prison. And they say they are trying to find me somewhere to live. My social worker will tell you everything. Will you talk to him? He's Norman Mills. He will tell you.'

I knew his number off by heart.

'And I'm going to go back to Wood End now. And I am going to be punished. I need you to speak to my social worker. That's the only reason I've run away, to see you. I need you to know that, that I haven't done anything wrong.'

He was taken aback, but friendly. He listened attentively and told me that he'd do his best but he couldn't make any promises. I never saw him again.

I was trying to kickstart the system in the same way that I had done with the psychiatrist, so I could get away from it. Back then, no one told me that it had worked. But it's here in my files.

SW
W.E. 19.10.8

Norman has approached Atherton Housing Department for a council tenancy and has made a favourable impression it appears. A Mr. Wilson has been in contact with Mr. Sumner (A.O.) regarding this, and it was therefore arranged that I would speak to Mr. Wilson also.

When I spoke to Mr. Wilson he confirmed that Norman could be offered a tenancy, despite his tender age, on the grounds that:

1. His is an exceptional case, and
2. he has a guarantor until his 18th birthday, and
3. there is enough evidence to support his application.

On this 3rd issue Housing would like a letter from me, to say that we believe Norman is capable of holding a tenancy. I questioned the 2nd part, re a guarantor, and Mr. Wilson said that this could be a friend or relative etc. Did not need to be this Authority. There is a possibility that Norman could be housed before Christmas this year.

182

When I returned to Wood End I was strip-searched and had my privileges taken from me. I could no longer turn the soil unsupervised. On 29 October the area officer, my social worker's line manager, wrote to the housing manager on his behalf.

Mr. N. Mills

KBS/NM/SW

29th October, 1984

The Housing Manager,
Housing Department,
Town Hall,
Atherton.

Dear Sir,

RE: LEMN SISSAY (D.O.B. 21.5.67) 'WOODEND' EVEREST RD., ATHERTON

I refer to my Senior Social Worker, Mr. Mills recent telephone call to your office, when he discussed the above named adolescent with Mr. Wilson of your Housing Dept.

Lemn as you are probably aware, has been in the care of this Authority virtually since birth. He was born in the Wigan area, and has spent the majority of his life in this locality, first with foster parents in Ashton in Makerfield, and in recent years in local Children's Homes, mainly in Atherton itself. He is a very intelligent and articulate young man, who is quite mature for his years, and who is decidedly capable of coping with a council tenancy should you feel able to offer this to him in the near future.

I would like to state therefore that I do support Lemn's application to your office for a tenancy. I would also like to point out that support will be available to this young man from this Department, not only until he leaves care on his 18th birthday, but beyond that time if he so wishes to accept it. As you are probably aware, Lemn has no blood relatives in this Country, and there is therefore no possibility of him finding alternative accommodation with a friend or relative etc. It would in my opinion be in Lemn's best interests to move to accommodation of his own, sooner rather than later.

I would like to thank you for the assistance you have given to Lemn in this matter.

Yours sincerely,

K. B. SUMNER
Are Officer

The area officer, Mr Sumner, wrote to the housing manager and the Assistant Director of Social Services on 26 and 29 October respectively.

opolitan Borough of Wigan

r-Departmental Memorandum

To Senior Assistant Director, HQ.	From Area Office, Golborne
Ref	Internal Telephone No: 32
	Ref KBS/MW

October 26th,1984

Re: Norman Greenwood known as Lem Sissay (d.o.b. 21.5.67)
Woodend Assessment Centre, Atherton.

Norman has now been resident in Woodend since June 1984. He is now 17½ years of age and obviously part of the ongoing plan for Norman has been to prepare him for leaving care and to assist him in obtaining accommodation for himself.

On his own initiative Norman has approached the Housing Dept at Atherton and has completed an application form for accommodation which seems to have been received with some encouragement. Norman has, at the Housing Departments request, written a letter outling his circumstances and his Social Worker has also had dialogue with a Mr Wilson of the Atherton Area Housing Office. It seems that Norman can get a private guarantor and no such demand will be made of this Department. However, since Norman is becoming increasingly restive at Woodend and delays are adding to irritations I wonder if representation through yourself to the Housing Department would speed matters up. Norman is self employed now and seems to have sown the seeds of reasonably steady business for the forseeable future. He is anxious to further his independence and obviously accommodation is his next step. Support from the Social Worker would continue beyond his 18th Birthday if Norman felt this necessary.

Any assistance you can give with this boys application to the Housing Dept would be appreciated.

AREA OFFICER

The J.G. Poyner below was Director of Wigan Social Services, responding against the advice of a senior social worker, an area manager and a housing manager to block my progress.

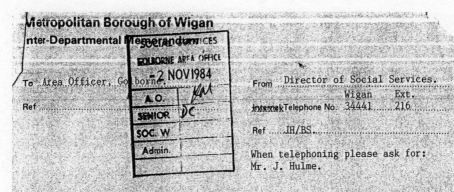

GOLBORNE AREA OFFICE

-2 NOV 1984

To Area Officer, Golborne.

Ref ....

A.O.

SENIOR   DC

SOC. W

Admin.

From Director of Social Services.

Wigan   Ext.

Internal Telephone No. 34441 216

Ref ..... JH/BS ....

When telephoning please ask for:
Mr. J. Hulme.

RE: NORMAN GREENWOOD, KNOWN AS LEMN SISSAY (D.O.B. 21.5.67) WOODEND ASSESSMENT
CENTRE, ATHERTON.

I acknowledge receipt of your memorandum of the 26th October, concerning the
above named and note with interest the future plans that you are developing
for this young man.

Having considered most carefully your proposal regarding a special approach
to a senior Officer of the Housing Department, I regret that I am unable to
comply with this request. However, I think it would be most appropriate if
you were to contact the relevant Housing Manager and acquaint him fully with
this young man's previous history, future plans and likely support that may
be necessary in the future.

Please keep my District Officer, Fieldwork Services acquainted with any future
developments.

J. G. Payner

31/10/84.

185

I am seeing this for the first time as I write. By mid-December 1984 I was in my flat. My first home. I was seventeen and a half. I lived on the newest housing development in Atherton. It was called Poets' Corner. My one-bedroom flat was at 21 Cowper Avenue. The streets that surrounded mine were Burns Avenue, Blake Avenue, Chaucer Grove, Keats Close, Byron Grove, Milton Close, Wordsworth Avenue, Browning Avenue. This whole housing area was being built while I was in the children's homes.

After thirty years, Graham Wilson, the housing officer, wrote to me out of the blue.

You probably won't remember me but if you cast your mind back to when you got your first flat on Poets' Corner (!) in Atherton I was the guy at the Atherton town hall who dealt with your application. You came in to see me a few times before you got the flat and I remember getting stick at the time as you were officially too young to have your own tenancy but I was impressed with you then and I have been really pleased to see how well things have worked out for you ever since. You deserve the recognition you now have. I left working for the council about a year after you got the tenancy (never was a local authority type!) but I remember how strong your character was then and the funny things you did eg Rasta colours on the front door! – Bowling ball games on the floor that your neighbour downstairs wasn't impressed with! – Walking round with the ladders on doing the gutters! and especially once when you left my office and I saw you through the window of the town hall when the motorcycle cop wasn't impressed with your 'holding the nose' gesture and he reacted badly!

I found this in my files relating to that incident.

Name.................. NORMAN SISSAY .... Case No.

REMARKS	Initials
Letter to Mr. Wilson supporting Normans housing appLciation. Mr. Poynter ha also been involved in discussion with Mr. Sumner on the matter of Norman being rehoused.	SW 29.10.84
Returned to work after leave, and discovered that Norman is to appear in Leigh Magistrates Court on 19.11.84, for 'conduct likely to cause a breach of the peace'. Discussed with Peter Mills at Woodend who says that Norman gave an obscene gesture to a police motor cyclist. Policeman apparently spoke to the lad, and then drove off. However, Norman then was said to have repeated the behaviour (verbal or gesture not known). Policeman therefore arrested Norman and he has been charged. Mr. Sumner spoke to a Sgt. Foster, last week, and explained Normans colour consciousness which may be at the root of this incident (suggestion that police motor cyclist had said 'Come here, black man'). However, police are still prosecuting. Said to Peter Mills that I would call within the next week and see Norman, prior to his appearance in Court. Norman is still operating his business, and staff are trying to encourage him to buy his own equipment for the future.	5.11.84
N. MILLS. S.S.W.	

I was charged with being 'likely to cause breach of the peace'. The court hearing was 5 November 1984.

REMARKS	Initials

Norman is making a great effort to get his flat together - but is
still short of many essentials. I have told him to stay in today
because of next delivery of some items from Golborne area. Said I
would see him on 24.12.84 next.

Prepared a report for Mr Hulme which Mr Sumner did discuss with him   21.12.84
at Golborne Area Office. However, I understand that Mr H is still not
agreeable to providing a grant for Norman.

Visited Normans flat but he was not at home.   24·12-84

                    N Mills, SSWorker

Visited Norman at his flat. He has been receiving his Benefit from   8.1.85
Mr Hayes (DHSS) and Mr Wilson at Atherton Housing. Norman was very
disappointed when I told him of the decision of Senior Management
not to give him a grant towards the setting up of his new home. He
is still short of essentials i.e. pots, pans, curtain rails cleaning
materials, paint : I had arranged for a second hand washing machine
to be delivered - but this did not arrive with the YTS transport
apparently.

Norman is learning to cope with his budgetting at last he feels -
after tending to spend all his DHSS Benefit very rapidly initially.
He intends to start up his business as soon as he can and he will
liaise with DHSS to keep them informed of his earnings. Meanwhile
he seems to be developing an even busier social life. He is
staying in Manchester from wednesday to Thursday this week with
friends, but is also involved with a coloured musical group and
accompanies them on 'gigs' reading his poetry. He seems quite sure
that through his various contacts some of his poetry will be
published soon. I have always feared that he might become socially
isolated when he left Childrens Home but instead he seems to
acquire more friends all the time. There were two of his friends in the
flat when I called today.

Norman is making a real effort to turn his flat into a comfortable
home, and I feel that he needs to be encouraged and supported in
this. The decision of this authority to date to offer no financial help,
however minimal, it does seem very short sighted. This young man has
no family to turn to for support and has been in care all his life.
To that extent, this Authority are in loco parentis   and are the
only body who have any responsibility for Norman. I feel that we
will have let him down badly if we do not offer more tangible
help in the near future. I have arranged with Norman to introduce
him to his new social worker   Brian Morris on Friday 11.1.85

Confirmed this arrangement with Brian today.   10·1·85

                    N Mills, SSWorker

188

Somebody left a gift for me outside the flat. I don't know who. It was a thing of beauty to me: a black Olivetti typewriter with a waterfall of ebony finger pads, each ingrained with one mother-of-pearl letter.

Epilogue

Be the window at dawn
Be the light be the ocean
Be the calm post-storm
Be open

Click clack clack. I was alone, at eighteen, in an apartment on Poets' Corner. I had a letter from my mother dated 1968 and a birth certificate with my name: Lemn Sissay. All the names which came before – Norman, Mark and Greenwood – were created to hide me from my mother and from Ethiopia.

My mother is from the Amhara people of Ethiopia. It is a tradition of the Amhara to leave messages in the first name of the child. In Amharic the name Lemn means Why?

Acknowledgements

Jamie Byng, Francis Bickmore, Leila Cruickshank, Megan Reid and all in the Canongate family, Clare Conville and all in the Conville and Walsh family. Ethiopia Alfred, Jo Prince and Andy King, Sally Bayley, Jenni Fagan, Meseret Fikru, Markos Fikru, Sophie Willan, Dave Haslam and the Haslamites, Jo and Tom Bloxham, Whitney McVeigh, Suzette Newman, Linda Lines, Mark Attwood, Bobbi Byrne, Peter Libbey, Norman Mills, Hannah Azieb Pool, Helen Pankhurst, Alula Pankhurst, Parvinder Sohal, Lebo Mashile, Jude Kelly and Caroline Bird.